I0058350

Strattomics

Strategies and Tactics for Sustainable Growth of your Enterprise

Huw Morris

Copyright © 2016 Huw Morris
All rights reserved.
ISBN: 0993170846

ISBN-13: 978-0-9931708-4-3

DEDICATION

To all the individuals, who are committed to developing sustainable growth through the efficiency, effectiveness and engagement of the stakeholders in their enterprise.

ACKNOWLEDGMENTS

As I wrote this new, significantly expanded, version of Strattomics, I reflected again on the people who have helped me learn and given me opportunities to improve a broad spectrum of enterprises. This started with school in Hertfordshire and then college in Kent in the UK, before a variety of roles during my Royal Air Force career in the UK, Germany and the USA. Then later while at Business School at Henley, teaching in Somerset and while working with Andersen Consulting / Accenture, the Financial Reporting Council, LECG, FTI Consulting and my clients. Most recently as I develop Efficienarta, I continue to learn from a spectrum of interesting and diverse people of all ages and a rich variety of backgrounds.

Thank you all.

Table of Contents

Table of Figures

1 INTRODUCTION

"Businesses that are not innovative and agile and that do not possess a clear sense of purpose and a good reputation with their stakeholders are unlikely to remain successful and independently sustainable over the longer term."

The Board Charter – Promoting business in society March 2014

The impact of **technology**, the expectations of **society** and evolving **social norms** represent a breadth of challenges for business leaders. *"In the new world it is not the big fish which eats the small fish, it's the **fast fish** which eats the **slow fish**."*[1] As Clayton Christensen, the Harvard Business School Professor states:

---

[1] Schwab, K., *Are you ready for the technological revolution?*, World Economic Forum Paper, 19 February, 2015

"Executives must personally monitor the available intelligence on the progress of pioneering companies ....They cannot rely on the company's traditional channels for gauging markets because those channels were not designed for that purpose."[2]

The hypothesis behind this book is that flourishing enterprises:

- **excel** at their **current activities**,
- spot **changes in their markets** early and
- develop their **agility** to embrace the new threats and opportunities.

This necessitates ever more **effective engagement** with employees and the full spectrum of an enterprise's **stakeholders**. Competitive advantage or new business streams can flow from ideas from anywhere within enterprises, but only if the **culture encourages people** to spot opportunity and if the managers recognise them. I feel strongly that it is the **role** of every Director and Manager to do this so that they lay a foundation for **sustained enterprise growth**.

I like to relate the development of businesses to expeditions through mountain ranges. The **better we are at the basics**, the quicker we can climb each mountain without accidents. The fitter we

---

[2] Christensen, C.M., *The Clayton M. Christensen Reader,* Harvard Business School Publishing Corporation, 2016.

are, the **more alert we are to changes** in our environment and the greater our capacity to **take in** more. More than just concentrating on putting one foot in front of the other. The **more agile** we are, the better we can respond to **new peaks** as they emerge. The **more robust our relationships** with our stakeholders, the more latitude we will be given if conditions mean changes to our plan.

This book includes a selection of **practical tools** and techniques and **integrates a spectrum management theory,** that I have used to improve business performance. I hope that these will help business leaders to think more effectively about their businesses; moreover, that they will help business leaders to retain (in the words of the Economist) "cool heads", as they climb the mountains of competition. The book endeavours to help leaders think about their business by enlarging **personal toolboxes** of business techniques, and by helping leaders **ask the right questions**. It has three central themes:

- **Continuous Improvement** of existing products and services (Enterprise Efficiency),
- **Raising agility** to promote proactive evolution of your business by spotting and embracing changes in your competitive environment (Enterprise Effectiveness),
- Positively **building stakeholder engagement** – amongst employees,

executives, non-executive directors, shareholders and local communities etc.

Throughout the book, tools and methods are introduced to engrain into your enterprise DNA, strategies, tactics and working practices to help **raise quality, grow agility and enhance relationships** with your full spectrum of stakeholders. I believe that action in these three areas increases the probability of **enduring competitive success**. The presentation of these techniques builds on Executive workshops that I have delivered over the last four years and the experience I gained during 30 years in management roles in private and public sector organisations. At the end of each chapter there is a link to electronic templates, job aids and other information relevant to the chapter.

For people who either use or are considering using management consultants, this book can also help you become a more effective buyer. Not least by helping you scope the particular areas where external assistance can add **the most value**.

"The competitive heat has been turned up by new technology. But cool heads are still needed when dealing with disrupters."

The Economist 11 January 2014

2 CONTINUOUS IMPROVEMENT

"Process Improvement is aligned around what our customers' value, which translates into business objectives that flow from the enterprise through the organization level down to individuals. .... We monitor a handful of key process metrics to ensure that we are making progress toward achieving corporate objectives. .... the ability to embrace change is not only core to continuous improvement but is indeed a foundation for competitive advantage."

GE (2014)

Most enterprises face intensely competitive environments, where customer expectations are becoming ever more demanding. Enterprises that have **continuous improvement** in their DNA, as opposed to a **we have always done it this way mentality**, have a better foundation for improving their competitiveness. They continuously **raise the bar** in meeting client expectations and **reduce their cost** of quality.   In his book *"Winners and* *how they succeed"*, Alastair Campbell (2015) quotes Sir David Brailsford, the Manager of the professional cycling Team Sky and Olympic winning British Cycling Team Coach:

"When you figure out that continuous improvement is going to be at the heart of everything you do, then your mind set is centred around that, full stop."

In this book I will introduce a number of tools and techniques for Managers to use as they climb to the next peak of their business journey. I believe that these are relevant to those responsible for delivering products and services of all kinds. Using these techniques can help raise the probability of successful improvements. They provide some structure to improvement efforts and include **practical steps** that are individually low risk (and consequently less fearful). The **prize**, is the ability to embrace continuous change as a **foundation for continuous improvement.** As mentioned in the quote at the beginning of this chapter, this can be a true competitive advantage. Furthermore it can **improve profitability** by reducing the cost of poor quality.

Quality

"Lasting improvements in performance depend on effort being applied in creating a particular sequence of capabilities and that these capabilities should be considered as cumulative developments, building on each other."

Ferdows and De Meyer (1990)

Quality, cost, dependability, speed and flexibility can all be targets for continuous improvement actions; however, operations research suggests that **quality** should be the first focus. Indeed the **Sandcone model of improvement** (Ferdows, K. in Brown, S.L, Eisenhardt, K.M., 1996) emphasises a sequential approach to performance improvement as shown in the following graphic.

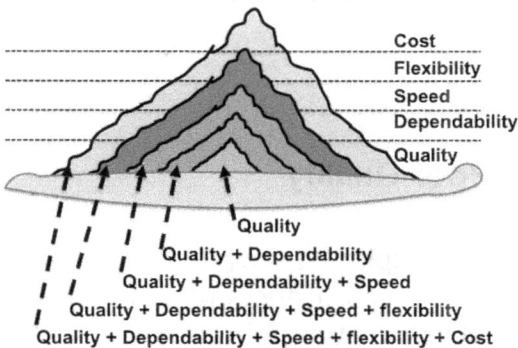

Figure 1: The sand-cone model

The **sand-cone analogy** is used to emphasise that the foundation for improvement must be continually widened to support increasing height). On the basis of this research, **quality performance** is a precondition to all lasting improvement. When an operation or process has reached an acceptable quality standard, the focus moves to identify actions to raise the level of dependability. In addition to implementing actions to improve dependability further improvements in quality continue to be sort. The same approach is then extended to the higher layers of the sand-cone, as each preceding level reaches an acceptable standard of performance. This is illustrated in the following graphic.

In the next two sections I will therefore start our continuous improvement journey with a focus on quality. I consider quality primarily from the perspective of customers for your offerings, irrespective of whether they are products or services.

Cost of Poor Quality

Before exploring practical continuous improvement steps, I encourage you to reflect on the **cost of poor quality** in an enterprise that you are familiar with.

Some costs such as the time taken to conduct inspections, the cost of re-work, scrap and warranty expenses are **visible.** Much of the cost of poor quality is however **hidden** below the waterline. Set-up costs for re-work, lost sales, poorer customer loyalty, increased volume of work-in-progress, management costs and more **volatile revenues** are less immediately apparent.

Figure 2: The Quality Iceberg

Clients

Can you list the clients for your products / services? I believe strongly that continuous improvement starts with gaining clarity about the clients you have and the **outcomes they are buying.** These can be in the external marketplace or internally within your enterprise. In their Harvard Business Review Article *The Elements of*

Value[3], Eric Almquist, John Senior and Nicholas Bloch point to the difficulty of nailing down **precisely what customers value**. They argue that traditional approaches are weak because they are based on testing "consumer reactions to preconceived concepts of value". Their research identified 30 "elements of value" that are segmented into 4 categories:

- Functional
- Emotional
- Life Changing
- Social Impact

Discussion of these elements of value is beyond the scope of this book; however, I urge you to think beyond the purely functional elements of your offerings when you consider the **benefits** being provided to your customers. For example, if you provide an expensive consumer good, one of the benefits to your customers may be the pleasure that they receive from being seen by their friends with your product.

Are you providing products and or services that fully meet the needs of your clients? If not, are you constrained by the current state of technology? For example, if you are providing information

---

[3] Almquist, A, Senior, J., Bloch, N., *The Elements of Value*, Harvard Business Review, September 2016.

systems that necessitate large volumes of data transfer, is the speed of the communications lines evolving too slowly? On the other hand, are you providing products or services that have significant functionality that your clients don't use? If you are, be particularly alert for new entrants to your market providing a cheaper option. What potential is there to **simplify** your products? In their book "Simplify: How the Best Businesses in the World Succeed", Richard Koch and Greg Lockwood argue that enterprises that successfully simplify follow one or other of the following two strategies (but most importantly they do not try to do both):

1. **Price Simplifying**. New, versions of a product or service that are dramatically cheaper to make while meeting the basic functional requirements of a customer. For example, low cost airlines have constructed their **simpler service** in a way that allows better utilisation of aircraft and outsources some of the work to passengers. As the price of air travel dropped significantly, the volume of flights increased massively, giving the low cost airlines rapidly increasing economies of scale.

2. **Proposition simplifying.** New products or services that are useful and very easy to use. For example Apple products that benefit from simplified designs that

minimise buttons, and embed user interfaces that enable customers to gain enjoyment quickly. This strategy creates new markets where customers may be prepared to pay a premium because the products or services are a pleasure to use.

Much of business has evolved from a world of **mass marketing**, where customers were considered as one group (or perhaps a series of segment groups), to one where technology and data allows us to strive to serve **markets of one**. I sense that these capabilities make understanding the diversity of customers, and the variety of outcomes that they are buying, increasingly important **critical success factors**.

Think for a moment about the **people or organisations** that **benefit** from the products or services that you and your team provide. I find it helpful to think holistically and to identify:

- The outcomes that your customers **buy**. As previously mentioned, this involves thinking broadly. Moreover, it necessitates developing a good understanding of how your customers use your product / service, ideally from **observation of their behaviour**.
- The suppliers that **feed** your business activity.

- The **inputs** that suppliers provide. These may be physical products, services or perhaps data of some kind that you then process.
- The process steps you use to **transform the inputs** into products or services.

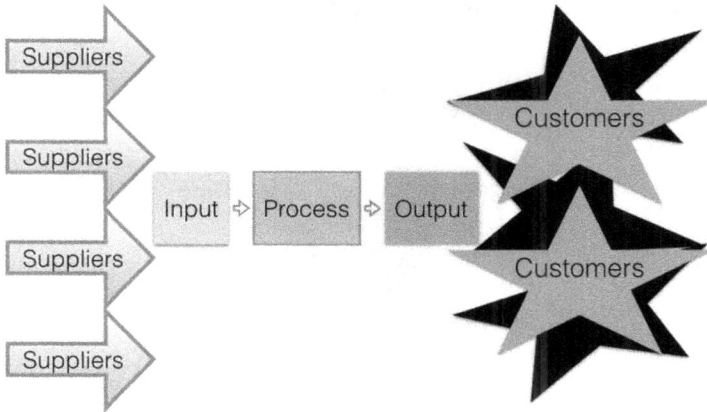

Figure 3: Suppliers, Inputs, Process, Outputs & Customers

Client Expectations

A theme running through a number of the cost of poor quality factors is a **gap** between the attributes of the service or product produced and the **expectations** of either your **client** or your own enterprise.

My premise is that a solid understanding of client expectations is the foundation for establishing the **dimensions** of the product or service you are providing. These dimensions comprise **scope**, the **people** delivering the product or service, the **time** taken to deliver, the **quality** and finally the **cost** (established from your assumptions for the first 4 "dimensions").

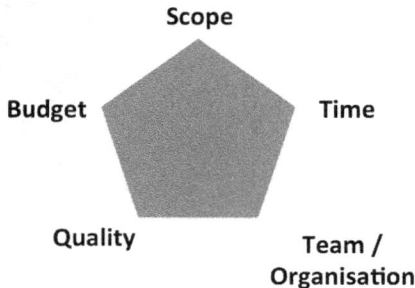

Figure 4: Project "dimensions"

Managing these dimensions of your offering, in alignment with your **client's expectations**, provides a foundation for satisfying client requirements. You may like to think of this in the context of **Performance – Expectations = Satisfaction**[4]. I acknowledge that developing a sufficient understanding of client expectations is easier said than done. I have developed a habit of asking probing questions to gain an **in-depth**

---

[4] Expectations Are Funny Things – CX Journey™ 5 April 2016. Available from: http://www.cx-journey.com/2016/04/expectations-are-funny-things.html

understanding of how the client will use our products and services. Provided that the client agrees, I make a note of **stated expectations** during meetings. Ideally, these meeting will include a variety of the client's people. My focus includes questions to develop a sense of their **unstated expectations**. One approach to identifying these unstated expectations is to map out **the journey** the customer experiences from their first contact with your enterprise to the point where their usage of your product or service ends. This **map** should capture the client's emotional highs and lows. Questions that identify the reasons for the highs and lows can provide further valuable insights into clients unstated expectations.

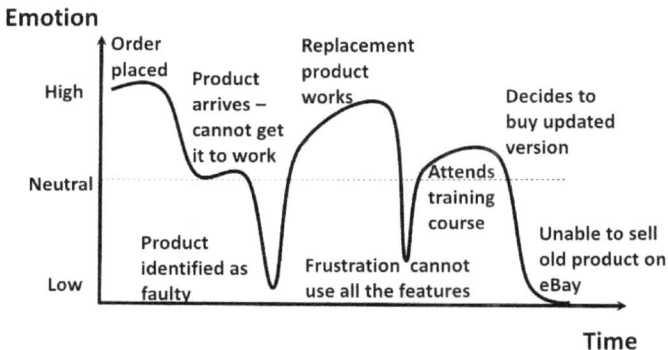

Figure 5: A client's emotional journey

Thinking about how **the client's clients** use the product or service that is going to incorporate the offerings may spark further questions. In my company, when a delivery team considers an expectation to be unrealistic, we consider **alternative approaches** that could meet the client need. We then discuss these with the Client to seek an **agreement** to the alternative. Having confirmed these expectations with the Client, the challenge is to put in place a plan to meet them at an **acceptable cost**. I will return to this in the Critical to Quality discussion below.

#	Expectation	Alternative Expectation (If unrealistic expectations have been gathered think about alternatives that would support a win/win)	Action

Figure 6: Expectation Matrix

I have used a similar expectation gathering approach to help me meet the expectations that my own boss has had for me. For example, a person I directly reported to, but saw rarely (he was based on the other side of the Atlantic ocean), was exceptionally busy but nonetheless had an expectation that I keep him up to date on the issues I was working on. The volume of emails was such that we considered other options. Our conclusion was a mix of concise voicemails that he could listen to when driving to work and instant messages for urgent items.

Critical to Quality

Having established an understanding of the client expectations and in particular how the Client **perceives value** (their vision of a successful outcome), the next step is to consider the factors that are critical to the quality of **meeting each expectation**. For example if a client expects that urgent product support questions are answered within 5 hours (300 minutes) it is important for those dealing with support questions to know this. Moreover the team concerned needs to be encouraged to put in place a **process** for **meeting** these **expectations**.

Following Peter Drucker's (1996) observation that **what gets measured gets done**, agreeing an appropriate measure and a **performance standard** is also prudent. When considering performance standards, I consider whether a target that is more demanding than the agreed performance standard should also be set (as an incentive for continuous improvement). **Target setting** has in my view elements of both art and science; however, I am always keen to **avoid averages**. The client in this case feels the variation in the time taken to deal with urgent support questions and an average measure may well **hide** some **totally unacceptable**

performances. For example some urgent requests may only take one minute. If there are 300 of these, 200 requests that take 5 minutes, 250 that take 10 minutes, 1 that takes 20 minutes and 1 that takes 500 minutes the average time taken will be under 4 minutes. This average is inside the response time required but masks one unacceptable response that took 500 minutes. In this case I would brainstorm with my team what percentage of urgent support questions they believe could be answered in 300 minutes in future. Depending upon the answer I would then consider whether **additional resources** may be necessary and if so what the **cost implications** would be. I would then discuss a target that we would use to promote **continuous improvement**.

A similar approach can be used to address the requirements of **other stakeholders**. For example, in a professional services firm the Partners may have a particular focus on securing prompt payment for the partnership's services. A popular metric used to give this a focus is **Days sales outstanding** (DSO). A critical to quality factor from the partnership perspective may be that DSO on each client account is less than 60[5].

Periodic reviews of the critical to quality factors with the relevant stakeholders can be a good way

---

[5] 60 would be driven by up to 30 days to bill the work and standard payment terms of 30 days.

of **validating** whether the enterprise is focusing its resources appropriately. It is useful to keep in mind that expectations change so this is not an unnecessary bureaucratic distraction. Some years ago I recall hearing an example from a kitchen catering for senior employees in a business. Knowing that the Company Chairman liked steak pies the chef directed that there would always be a steak pie immediately available should the Chairman arrive for lunch. This **waste of resources** only surfaced as an issue some years later when a subsequent chef was asked why there was always one steak pie in stock. It transpired that the Chairman had retired a couple of years previously so by no stretch of the imagination could having a steak pie in stock be considered critical to the quality of the service provided by the kitchen.

Critical to Process

Building on the **critical to quality** product support example above, my next step would be to identify the critical to process factors. These are the activities that would need to be delivered in order to achieve the critical to quality requirements i.e. that urgent product support questions are answered within 300 minutes. These might include:

- **Logging** all support requests within 30 minutes and categorizing those urgent for special handing.
- **Escalating** urgent support requests to the appropriate individual within 45 minutes.
- Escalating any unanswered urgent requests to the **line manager** after 200 minutes.

After considering the **critical to process** steps required to achieve the performance identified as critical to quality, I review the feasibility of consistently achieving the level of service expected. If this is in doubt I will arrange a meeting with the client to consider options. These may include a proposal to agree a performance standard that would expect 95% of urgent support requests to be addressed in less than 300 minutes. My next step will be to create a client service dashboard that shows:

- The **volume** of support requests.
- The **number** classified **urgent**.
- Our performance in meeting the **performance standard**.
- A **narrative explanation** for the urgent requests not met within 300 minutes.

This **dashboard** would then be shared with the client, ideally on line **in real time**. It would then be used as a basis for regular performance reviews.

Turning to the less than 60 Days Sales Outstanding (that was considered **critical to quality** by the professional services firm Partners), critical to process steps could include:

- An **explicit term** in Client contracts requiring invoices to be paid within 14 days.
- Identifying the person at the client who **approves invoices** for payment.
- All individuals working on client projects reporting the time spent on each project weekly.
- Monthly invoices being prepared for Client Partner approval on **working Day 1** of each month.
- Approved invoices being submitted to the person responsible for approval on **working Day 2** of each month.

Enterprises such as[6] Motorola, GE, Dow and a spectrum of Financial Services have extended this critical to quality and critical to process thinking into a robust implementation of Six Sigma metodology. This is a quality improvement approach that defines defects and statistically analyses these as a basis for reducing variation in performance. As part of my work as a Director of Operations at Accenture I used the Six Sigma approach to determine the measures we used to

[6] Pande, P.S. Newmann, R.P., & Cavenagh, R, 2000, The Six Sigma Way: How GE, Motorola, and Other Top Companies are Honing Their Performance, McGraw Hill.

promote continuous improvement of our business development and quality processes and subsequently in our intellectual property company.

Winning by Building Quality into Work

*"To win, you need genuine innovation, not imitation..........If I had one word to sum up our approach to innovation, it would be **iteration**."*

Paddy Lowe, Executive Director Mercedes F1 Team[7]

A combination of relevant, genuine innovation and a commitment to building quality into your products and services lays the foundation for continuous improvement. Back in 1961, Shigeo Shingo at Toyota implemented a system known as **Poke Yoke** to build quality into products by **error proofing** processes against mistakes. The mistake proofing approach recognized that human beings make mistakes and creates designs and systems that minimize or eliminate these. There are two components:

- Mistake prevention.
- Immediate mistake detection.

---

[7] Quoted by Alastair Campbell in his book Winners – How they Succeed (2015), pages 298 and 300.

When you refuel your car for example, you benefit from an **innovation** that has been refined by numerous designers and manufacturers. The size of the end of the fuel hose reduces the risk of putting leaded fuel into an unleaded car, the filler cap is generally attached to the car to reduce the risk of loss and the cap itself has a click mechanism to reduce the risk of over tightening it.

Turning to immediate mistake detection, The National Institute of Standard Technology published a study in 2002 that noted that the cost of fixing one bug found in the production stage of software is 15 hours compared to five hours of effort if the same bug is found at the coding stage. It is not therefore surprising that software development methodologies include **stage containment** steps that aim to identify errors before development moves to the next stage. A **similar approach** can be adopted in the development of **most products and services**. For example, when taking a customer order, checking the order quantities and other attributes before transmitting the order to the warehouse. Increasing use of digital technology such as Tablet Computers for taking orders opens up many new opportunities for mistake prevention. For example **validation** can be coded into the forms etc. This means **fewer opportunities** for incomplete or inaccurate data.

Process Sponsorship

Once a clear understanding has been developed of the steps that are critical to the achievement of the quality outcomes (as **perceived by the customer**), five immediate actions are then helpful:

1. Appoint an appropriately senior individual to be the **sponsor** of the process involved.
2. Identify who should be **accountable**, who should be **responsible**, who should be **consulted** and who should be **informed** at each step in the process. Note that only one person should be accountable for each step in a process. It is also helpful to identify where support can be obtained if an individual has difficulty with a particular process step. A Responsible, Accountable, Consult and Inform (**RACI**) matrix, such as the one below, can be used to **agree** and **communicate** these requirements.

Names:	AA= Adrian Alpha		AE=Andrew Echo	
	BB= Bert Beta		BF=Brian Foxtrot	
	CC=Charlie Charlie		CG=Chris Golf	
	DD=David Delta		DH=Derek Hotel	

Goal / Objective	Responsible	Accountable	Consulted	Informed
Objective 1	AA	CC	DD,AE	DH
Task 1	AA	CG	CC	DD, AE, DH
Objective 3	BB	CC	DD,AE,BF	DH

Figure 7: Responsible, accountable, consulted, informed, Matrix

3. Under the sponsor's direction, undertake an assessment of any **barriers** to implementation. For example, do any existing policies or procedures need to be amended? What tools (including job aids) could be developed to help people deliver the required quality outcomes **efficiently, effectively and consistently**. An example of a process job aid, designed to provide individuals with the full context of a process, is in the next section.

4. **Document** the current agreed process as a means of promoting a shared understanding, and as a foundation for identifying improvements.

5. Set a date for reviewing the process to establish whether it remains **fit for purpose**. During such process reviews it is important to consider the **impact** of changes in both the enterprise and the enterprise's business environment. In our agile world this is something that **merits attention more frequently** than in the more stable days of the past.

Consolidating the process maps created into a Process Library has proved to be a good foundation for consistently delivering quality products and services. Modern software[8] enables **digital process libraries** to be developed and maintained efficiently. No longer are the administrative burdens such as printing and hand written amendments a deterrent to **continuous improvement**.

Applying the Sand cone approach

Returning to the Sand cone model introduced at the beginning of Chapter 2, it is now time to broaden the improvement focus beyond quality. In the following section I include four examples to illustrate how **innovations** in your industry may well flow from successful innovations and **practices elsewhere**. Indeed industries that may be far removed from your activities.

---

[8] For example the Process Library solution developed by Triaster – details available from
http://processlibraries.triaster.co.uk/Triaster%20Browser%20Toolkit%20201
1/MobileHomepage/frames.aspx?sitetype=click&library=processlibrary&site
=live

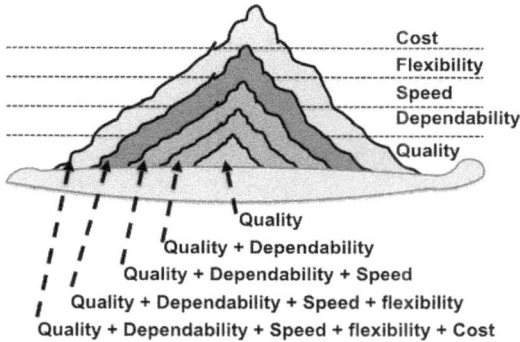

Figure 8: The sand-cone concept

1. In a space mission a repair after launch is frequently impossible and component failures can consequently lead to unrecoverable consequences. **Dependability** requirements are therefore a particularly critical attribute alongside overall quality criteria. Even in this environment, a dependability programme can be a **hard sell** because it does not generate physical products or services and the outputs of a dependability programme are generally recommendations on design trade-offs, a statement of risk, a procurement choice or identification of potential design weaknesses. The potential benefits may be far in the future and decision makers may consequently discount these too heavily. Turning to more mass-market products and services the broad

adoption of Six Sigma[9] indicates the value that industry places on reducing the level of variation in processes (and hence increasing their dependability).

2. McLaren Applied Technologies (an offshoot of the Formula 1 Motor Racing Team) has used the thinking from Formula 1 pit stops, where 4 wheels can be changed in 2.3 seconds, with GlaxoSmithKline to improve the efficiency of toothpaste production lines.[10] These production lines consistently achieved quality requirements but suffered lost production of 39 minutes each time the product being produced was changed. Using a fast but not hurried principle from pit stops, speed has been improved by reducing the time to change products to 15 minutes. This enables 24 minutes of additional production each time a product change is implemented. Moreover it improves agility as it makes smaller production volumes for each product economic.

---

[9] In both traditional manufacturing and in services. The research by Alessandro Laureani, Juju Antony and Alex Douglas *Lean six sigma in a call centre* demonstrated that six sigma can make a positive contribution to continuous improvement by, for example, increasing first-call resolution, reduction in operator turnover and streamlining of processes.

[10] Quoted by Alastair Campbell in his book *Winners – How they Succeed* (2015), pages 303.

3. Supermarkets may identify check out queues as a barrier to securing more business. Actions to reduce the magnitude of this issue may include more **flexibility** for customers and amongst the staff. For example customers may be given the option of a **self-service check out**[11], or self-scanning of products (to reduce the time needed at the check out). Staff with duties around the store, or indeed in the back office, may be given training so that they can operate checkouts at busy times. This added flexibility enables the store to adjust more efficiently to short, unpredictable periods of increased business.

4. Delivering Internet ordered groceries to peoples' homes is another activity benefiting from investments made by a Formula One racing team. To improve driving skills and reduce fuel consumption, Sainsbury's supermarket drivers in the United Kingdom are using the computer-based simulation programs developed by the Williams Formula 1 team. This is expected to result in fuel **cost** savings of up to 30 per cent.

"Formula 1 is well recognized as an excellent technology incubator. It makes perfect sense to embrace some of the

---

[11] Using systems such as the ones described in this MIT document: http://web.mit.edu/2.744/www/Project/Assignments/humanUse/lynette/2-About%20the%20machine.html

*new and emerging technologies that the Williams
Technology Centre in Qatar is developing to help
Sainsbury's mission to reduce its energy consumption."*

Williams F1's Former Chief Executive, Alex Burns.[12]

Returning to the **Sand cone concept** unless cost reduction is a main strategic theme of the business, one would not make cost reduction decisions that negatively impact the quality (as perceived by the customer), speed, dependability or flexibility of the overall operation.

Enterprises that place a premium on effective learning are better equipped to institutionalise the steps need to build quality into their processes. Slack et al (2015) emphasises a goal of **double loop learning**. A first step can be clarifying exactly what the client is buying, as discussed earlier. Rather than focusing purely on minimising the defects in a process:

*"...double loop learning questions the fundamental
objectives, service or even the underlying culture of the
operation. This kind of learning implies an ability to challenge
existing operating assumptions in a*

---

[12] Quoted by in Slack, N, Brandon-Jones, A, Johnston, R, 2015, *Operations Management*, 7th Edition. Pearson Higher Education (UK) 06/2017, VitalBook file.

fundamental way. It seeks to re-frame competitive assumptions and remain open to any changes in the competitive environment."

Slack et al (2015)

Perhaps one of the more difficult elements of this for management is to embrace the need to **abandon existing routines** in order to exploit new opportunities successfully. In the next section I will take the next step in our journey up the mountain and focus on continuous improvement.

An example Job Aid
Purpose:

The Company X accounts payable process facilitates pre-approval of business expenditure within agreed delegations, appropriate approvals of invoices & expenses and timely payment through the banking system.

Process Diagram:

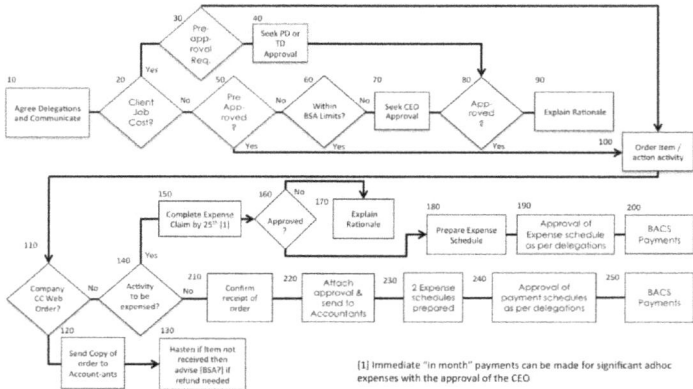

[1] Immediate "in month" payments can be made for significant adhoc expenses with the approval of the CEO

Process Description (A key to appointments is below the table):

[1] Responsible [2] Accountable [3] Consulted [4] Informed

Step	Description	Res(1)	Acc (2)	Con (3)	Inf (4)
10	Discuss, agree and communicate authorities to approve 1. Expenses that will be billed and collected from clients, 2. Other Client job specific costs, 3. Routine General Administrative costs (up to XXX), 4. Staff Expenses.	CEO	CEO	PD, TD, BSA	
20	Segment costs between those that are related to delivering sold work and other costs.				
30	TD and PD set criteria for Pre Approval of job delivery related costs	TD / PD	TD / PD		
40	For Professional Services, jobs seek approval of TD for costs related to delivery of client jobs e.g. travel, xxx, xxx. For Software implementations seek approval of PD for implementation related costs.	Requester	TD / PD		
50	Establish whether the Sales or General Administrative cost concerned has already been approved	Requester	CEO	TD / PD	Requester
60	Establish whether the cost concerned can be approved by the BSA	Requester	BSA	TD / PD	Requester
70	Email CEO with request for approval of costs for item / service needed	Requester	BSA	TD / PD	Requester
80	Expenditure request considered	CEO	CEO	TD / PD	Requester
90	If request is not being approved, explain to the requester the reasons	CEO	CEO		Requester
100	Order item (from standard supplier if appropriate) / service, engage in activity (e.g. Travel)	Requester	Requester	CEO	BSA
110	Company Credit Card Order?	Requester	Requester		
120	If Company credit card used,	Requester	Requester		

	send copy of order to Accountant by email				
130	Make a diary reminder to ensure receipt of item / service is confirmed	Requester	Requester		
140	If individual has mileage expenses or personally paid for the item / activity / service it expense as soon as possible	Requester	Requester		
150	Complete the company mileage or expense form by 25th of the month	Requester	Requester		
160	Approval of expense claim in accordance with delegations	TBC	CEO		TD / PD
170	If request is not being approved, explain to the requester the reasons	CEO	CEO		Requester
180	Prepare Schedule of approved expenses submitted by staff	BSA	BSA		
190	Approval of expense schedule in accordance with delegations approved by CEO. NOTES: 1. Any novel or in anyway non-standard payments should be approved personally by the CEO. 2. With the exception of the CEO, employees are not authorised to approve payments to themselves.	BSA	BSA CEO	CEO	CEO
200	Make Bank Payment	BSA	CEO		
210	Confirm receipt of item on the invoice or copy of order and pass to the approver	Requester	Requester		BSA
220	Email copy of invoice / order to accountant with approval	App	App		BSA
230	Prepare schedules of payments for approval: A. Payments that can be approved by the BSA by 30th of the month, B. Schedule of all other payments for approval of the CEO by working day zzz of the month	PA	PA	CEO	BSA
240	Approval of payment schedules in accordance with delegations approved by CEO. NOTES: 1. Any novel or non-standard	BSA / CEO	CEO	CEO	

	payments should be approved personally by the CEO. 2. With the exception of the CEO, employees are not authorised to approve payments to themselves.				
250	Make Bank (BACS) Payment	PA	PA	CEO	CEO

APP   Approver - in accordance with delegations

BSA   Business Support Administrator

PA   Accounting

PD   Product Director

PD   Product Director

PEM   Product Engagement Manager

Figure 9: Example Process Map & Job Aid

Continuous Improvement

*"Amazon invests a lot of time and money in "flywheels;" innovating the things that don't seem too obvious, but are actually really obvious. Flywheels are those things that **never change** for the customer like price, convenience, delivery time and the size of catalogue. It's impossible to imagine a future 10 years from now where customers wish the prices were a little higher, or delivery was a bit slower..."*

Jeff Bezos CEO Amazon[13]

The most successful businesses are those that focus energy on **adapting through innovation** rather than innovating through adapting (Campbell, 2015). This involves constantly asking questions about **what** you are doing and **why**. Then considering whether there is a better way of meeting your customer needs and one that is better than your competition:

"Marginal gains means looking at all the things we do, and never assuming we couldn't do them better."

Dave Brailsford [14]

---

[13] Datafox Blog, 16 February 2014, http://www.datafox.co/blog/2014/02/jeff-bezos-fireside-chat/

[14] Quoted by Alastair Campbell in his book *Winners – How they Succeed* (2015)

This section contains established tools to help you identify areas for continuous improvement and then consider the most critical human dimension of continuous improvement.

Plan, Do, Check, Act

However well you have designed your activities, and built quality into your processes, there is likely to be potential for **continuous improvement**. Focusing resources on securing such improvements, should increase the satisfaction of your customers and other stakeholders, including employees and investors. One approach originates from the 1920s work of a statistician by the name of Walter Shewhart[15]. He developed the **statistical process control** technique in the Bell Laboratories in the United States of America. Subsequently this thinking was embedded into the Quality movement pioneered by W Edwards Deming in the 1950s. At its core is a **Plan, Do, Check, Act (PDCA) cycle** that is sometimes known as the Deming Wheel.

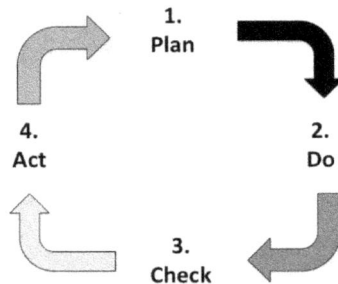

Figure 10: Plan, Do, Check, Act (PDCA) Cycle

The checking step may include:

- Measurements introduced when considering the **critical to process factors**, identified as central to delivering products or services that **meet the quality expectations of customers**.
- Sophisticated statistical process control techniques.[16]

After the PDCA cycle has been completed, the standard level of performance of the activity concerned should be higher. Over time, repeated

---

[16] Mohammad Hossain of the University of North Texas provides a chronological explanation of the development of Statistical Process Control in his short paper *Development of Statistical Quality Control: Evolution or Revolution*, available from:
http://www.academia.edu/2457002/DEVELOPMENT_OF_STATISTICAL_Q UALITY_CONTROL_EVOLUTION_OR_REVOLUTION

PDCA cycles can have a very material impact on the quest to improve enterprise performance **faster** than your competitors.

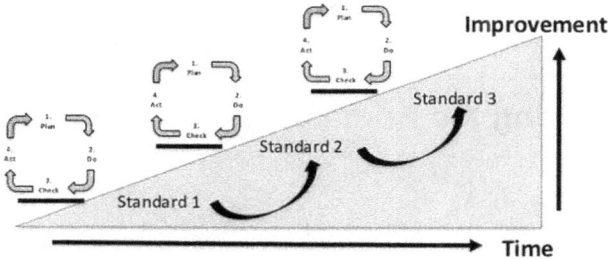

Figure 11: Progressively raising performance

This well-established method has stood the test of time. It is a required approach in some organisations. In some cases this is a consequence of the quality standards that they are certified to. For example the old 2005 ISO27001 standard (*Information technology - Security techniques - Information Security Management Systems - Requirements*)[17] mandated it. In my experience, keys to **securing value** from this, and other quality management techniques are to:

---

[17] Details available from:
http://www.iso.org/iso/catalogue_detail?csnumber=42103

a. Keep the **focus** on the **changing needs of the customer**.
b. **Avoid** building a mass of **bureaucracy** around the core idea of planning, doing and checking. Such bureaucracy can in itself become a barrier to agility.

Identifying the Root-cause of performance issues

Human beings have a tendency to ask questions that they think they may have an immediate answer to, notwithstanding that a more difficult question would undercover more valuable insights (Kahneman, 2011). The ever-increasing volume of data in our Internet connected world, puts an increasing premium on asking the right questions. The easy questions are more likely to expose symptoms of issues rather than root-causes. The effort involved in framing more **probing questions** is consequently likely to be rewarded with deeper insight into the drivers of particular issues.

The **5 Whys** technique can be an effective approach to structuring analysis to identify the root-cause of a performance issue. The technique was formalised as part of the Toyota Production System and is now in widespread use as part of Kaizen, Lean manufacturing, Six Sigma and other quality management approaches. For example, a customer for a project to transfer an archive of enterprise data from their servers to a cloud service may raise a complaint. In this case the **iterative process** of asking **5 questions** may establish that:

1. Why - the project running behind schedule.
2. Why - the project team have identified more work than in the original plan.
3. Why – the validation of data prior to transfer to the cloud is failing.
4. Why - many incidents of data corruption have been found.
5. Why – client staff turnover has been high and the individuals currently involved have not been maintaining the servers containing legacy data. This is necessitating collection of back up data from an external back up service provider.

One tool for facilitating robust analysis of **root-causes** is the fishbone or Ishikawa diagram (named after Kaoru Ishikawa who pioneered quality techniques in the Kawasaki shipyards in Japan). This tool is a favourite of management consultants because it is an effective way of **identifying** the **potential factors** causing an overall effect and then **communicating** these **visually to stakeholders**. Causes (reasons for imperfection) are generally segmented according to the source of the variance. For example, for an analysis of a manufacturing issue the following segmentation may be appropriate:

- People
- Methods – including procedures
- Machines
- Materials
- Metrics i.e. Data used to evaluate the quality of the process(es) being used
- Environment

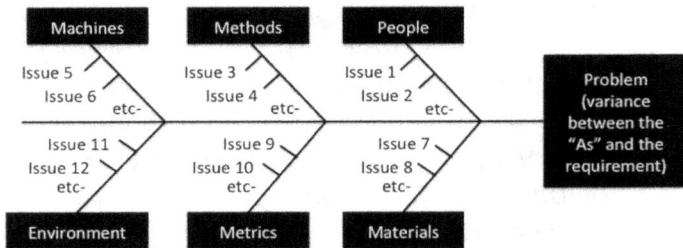

Figure 12: Manufacturing Issue Ishikawa (Fishbone) diagram

If the issue is in a marketing activity the segmentation could be:

- Product / Service
- Positioning
- Price
- Place
- Promotion
- People
- Packaging

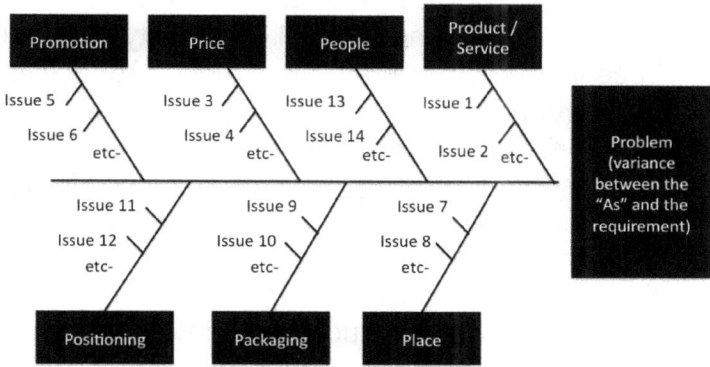

Figure 13: Marketing Issue Ishikawa (Fishbone) diagram

Encouraging Ideas

"There is no copyright on to new ideas"

José Mourinho[18]

The continuous improvement discussion has so far been based on meeting customer expectations. I am now going to extend the discussion to consider the **benefits** that can be gained from **involving staff**. This includes proactive efforts to

---

[18] Quoted by Alastair Campbell in his book *Winners and how they succeed* (2015). José Mourinho, the Manager of Manchester United Football Club, went on to observe that "There is so much technology, everyone knows everything about everyone......Someone can produce something, a new idea, which then becomes fundamental and there is no copyright. So you must innovate all the time. You must always be thinking of where things are changing".

improve the business in ways that may not necessarily be seen immediately by customers or show up in existing Critical to Quality, Critical to Process metrics or Plan, Do, Check, Act activities. Justin King, the former CEO of Sainsbury's (a large UK Supermarket chain) says that it is not about trying **anything** - it is about knowing your purpose, what you are **trying to achieve**. How you behave when innovation fails will tell people all they need to know whether your serious about innovating or not. To quote Justin King[19]:

"Celebrate it when it is successful, reward it when it is successful; and learn from failure by not making the same mistakes twice."

When working with enterprises, I now integrate a purpose statement into a **strategic diamond**. This promotes a line of sight from purpose through strategic themes to initiatives, measures and targets. I find it particularly helpful to consider the **implications** of **measures** and **targets** being discussed for the elements higher up the diamond. This can help staff, including those at junior levels, know more about what the **enterprise** is trying **to achieve**.

---

[19] Quoted by Alastair Campbell in his book *Winners and how they succeed* (2015)

Figure 14: Efficienarta Strategic Diamond with explanation

If the people in your organisation share a **sense of purpose** and are aware of the **strategic themes** they will already know what you are trying to achieve. They are therefore well placed to contribute to efforts to embrace innovation. Don't avoid angry people as they can be the most energetic spotters of **innovative ideas** (Peters, 2010). Ron Ashkenas (2014), in his Harvard Business School Blog *"Even Good Employees Hoard Great Ideas"*, articulated the challenge of incentivising individuals to share their ideas. The evidence on the effectiveness of financial incentives is mixed; however, enterprises with **leaders who are trusted** and **show commitment** to developing new ideas, have a stronger foundation for surfacing innovate ideas from both individuals and teams. Ashkenas recommends that enterprises start their journey towards a more innovation-friendly culture by:

1. **Educating people** about what innovation means for their enterprise[20],
2. Building **innovation into goal-setting** and performance management processes,
3. Finding and **publicising** some early **examples** of innovation, where people did the **right things in the right ways** and created new value for the enterprise.

In my experience there are thee critical success factors in the early stages of initiatives to generate **innovative** ideas. Enterprise leaders need to **transparently prioritise the ideas**, be seen to **invest in the best** and **explain** why any proposed initiatives are not developed. With modern software, enterprises can capture and evaluate ideas without creating a bureaucratic nightmare. The Financial Times (2014) article *"Idea Management Software Boosts Collaboration"* provides concise examples of enterprises using idea generation software and suggests that the "simplicity of the software will encourage companies to take up the challenge". As Mr Geyer of MetLife states in the article, **giving employees the chance** to take part in the development of the company is good for morale.

---

[20] As Clayton Christensen (2016) emphasises "Sustaining innovation maintains a steady rate of product improvement".

"People who've been with us 25 years say this is first time they've really felt valued, engaged with the direction of the company, and that management has considered their ideas."

Initiating changes

"Sometime wonderful changes come about naturally, accidentally, or completely out of the blue. But change making doesn't always happen by chance. You need to have the right environment, tools, support and attitude to become a change maker."

Richard Branson (2013)

Once you have **scoped-out an innovative idea** or identified the **root-cause of a problem** (the variance between the "As Is" and the level of performance required to meet customer expectations), **resources** will be **needed for implementation**. Hopefully your enterprise will have a wealth of improvement ideas and the initial challenge will be to decide **which ideas** merit **implementation** resources. Enterprises that use their strategic objectives to prioritise initiatives are more likely to obtain **sustained top management sponsorship**.

Having decided on which improvement initiatives to **resource**, action will need to be initiated. Before deciding on the action, consideration of factors that will **impact on the change** can help you shape and position the change effort. Such discipline makes implementation more likely to be successful. In this section I will introduce 3 techniques to your **back-pack of tools** to help you shape and prioritise improvement actions. Later in the Raising Agility chapter, we discuss the importance of considering unintended consequences of change initiatives:

Force Field Analysis

Kurt Lewin of the University of Iowa, one of the early writers on **Change Management**, suggested that it is helpful to think about the propagators (**driving forces**) and inhibitors (**blockers**) of change when **shaping actions**. He recognised that building on the driving forces alone would generally increase the inhibitors of change. He termed this technique **Force Field Analysis**.

You can implement a Force Field Analysis using the following steps:

1. Define the outcome of the change in a short statement.

2. List the personal, interpersonal, inter-group, cultural, administrative, technological, environmental and any other factors, that will drive the change needed to achieve the outcome.

3. List the personal, interpersonal, inter-group, cultural, administrative, technological, environmental and any other, factors that will restrain the change needed to achieve the outcome.

4. Consider each of these forces in turn to identify how influential / strong each one is. How much, if any, control do you have over each of the forces? Are there connections between the forces i.e. if you influenced one would it affect another?

5. Rank those that you can influence in order of importance.

6. Identify practical actions you could take that will:

    a. Build on driving forces.
    b. Reduce resisting forces.

For example, you may face the following in an opportunity to expand the scope of services you supply to a public sector client:

Forces supporting change	Forces opposing change
External	
Government pressure for change →	← Political opposition to a more commercial approach
De-regulation →	← Client unions
Demand for Price reductions →	
Increasing Competition →	← Lack of funding
Internal	
Established project capability →	← Poor communication ← Poor support from senior client management.
Highly engaged, quality staff →	
Positive attitude to change →	← Low client motivation ← Ineffective client Leadership

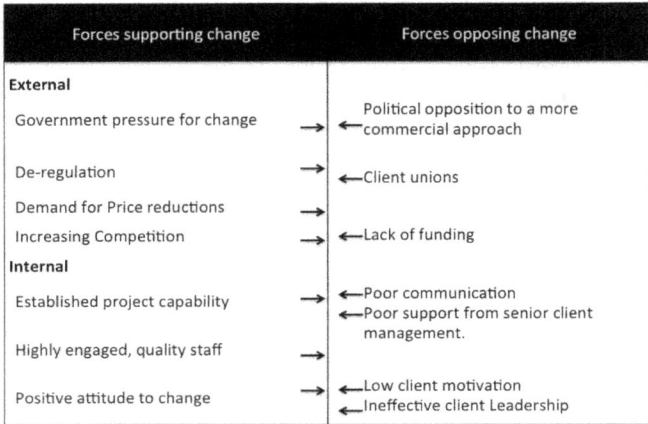

Figure 15: Force Field Analysis - Stage 1

Following a conversation where the age and reliability of the current file storage is mentioned as a major concern, you decide to produce a proposal to provide the client with cloud based file storage. A **brainstorming workshop** with your colleagues highlights the following assessment of **driving forces** and **blockers**:

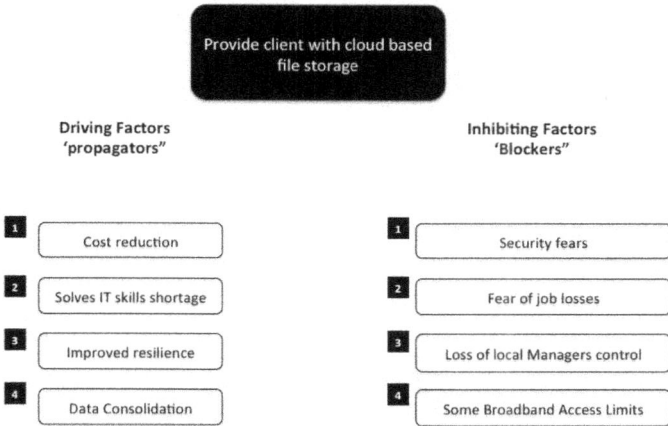

Figure 16: Force Field Analysis - Stage 2

The aim is now to **minimise** the impact of the **blockers** by **exploiting** the **propagators**. At a personal level, behavioural economics can help us optimise the effectiveness of our actions[21]. Following further internal discussion you decide on

---

[21] For example, in the United Kingdom there is concern that individuals are not contributing enough to their future pensions. A decision to have a process that involved individuals having to take an action to "opt-out" of contributions rather than "opting-in" has increased materially the level of pension contributions.

the following actions:

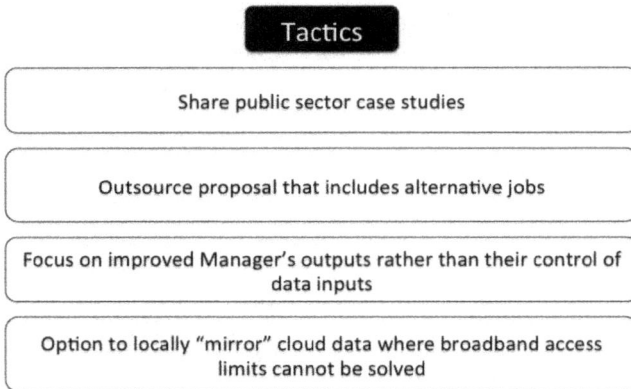

Figure 17: Force Field Analysis - Stage 3

Effective / Attainable Analysis

When considering how to address business improvement opportunities, more than one option is usually identified. Before conducting some form of financial cost benefit analysis it can be helpful to **rank the options** on the basis of **effectiveness and attainability**.

For example, in an enterprise I used to work with, the time taken for clients to pay invoices was increasing. This increase in receivables from clients, was both hurting cash flow and increasing operational costs. (The enterprise used Economic-

Value-Added as one of the key measures of organisational performance and optimising free cash flow was a priority). The following options for reducing client receivables were tabled in a discussion amongst the Leadership Team:

a. **Advance bill** clients for our services (with a modest discount for prompt payment).

b. Reduce the **time** taken to **issue invoices**.

c. **Hand-deliver** invoices to the **person responsible** for approving them for payment and invite them to **highlight** immediately **any issues** they have with the invoice.

d. **Hasten** overdue invoices more frequently and escalate non-payment earlier, for **follow up** by more senior staff.

e. **Stop work** on projects where **invoices are overdue**.

f. **Reduce payment terms** on new engagements from 30 days to 14 days.

Following the discussion, the Chief Financial Officer (CFO) assessed the effectiveness of each of the suggestions as follows:

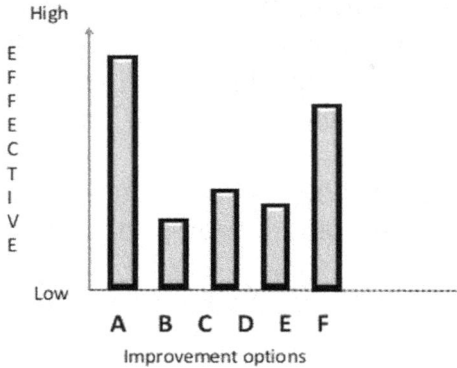

Figure 18: Comparison of the effectiveness of alternative improvement options

The CFO then had telephone conversations with three of the most experienced Account Managers and debated the attainability of each of the suggestions. Their conclusion was:

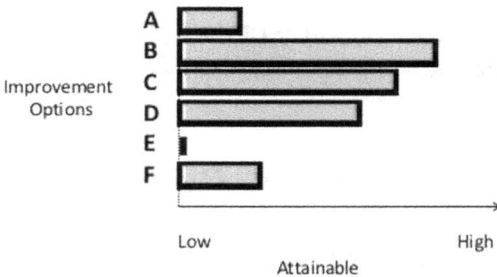

Figure 19: Comparing the attainability of different improvement options

Prior to the following Executive meeting the CFO circulated the following matrix to **provoke** further **discussion** and a **decision**.

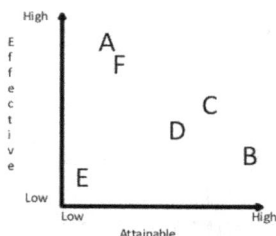

Figure 20: Effective - Attainable Analysis

The Executive Team decided to:

1. Build an advanced billing option into all new proposals (Option A).

2. Reduce standard payment terms to 14 days (Option F).

3. Hand-deliver invoices to the person responsible for approving them for payment and invite them to highlight immediately any issues they have with the invoice (Option C).

4. Hasten overdue invoices more frequently and escalate non-payment earlier for follow up by more senior staff (Option D).

Over the following year these actions had a material impact on improving the enterprise's free cash flow.

Importance Performance Matrix

In addition to considering the effectiveness and attainability of an improvement from the perspective of one's own enterprise, it is prudent to consider it from the **customer(s) viewpoint**.

Returning to the example used earlier in the Critical to Quality discussion[22], a proposal to introduce an automated "ticketing" system for support questions could be assessed on the basis of effectiveness and client satisfaction. I would approach this by:

1. Identifying the attributes of the solution that will impact the satisfaction of the customer's Critical to Quality (CTQ) factors. If there were any doubts about this I would check with the **customer**. The last thing I would want, is to **surprise** an important customer with a change in our processes **without any consultation**! For example, does the

---

[22] A customer who expects that urgent product support questions are answered by your enterprise within 5 hours.

customer value having on-line access to the status of their support questions?

2. Consider how important each of these attributes is to the Customer.

3. Assess how effectively you can satisfy the most important attribute.

4. Chart your assessment on an Importance - Performance Matrix showing the customer's satisfaction and your anticipated effectiveness in satisfying it.

For example, the **client may value** being able to see immediately on a web page, details of support calls not being cleared after 3 hours. The proposed **ticketing system** could easily provide this visibility without adding to your costs so:

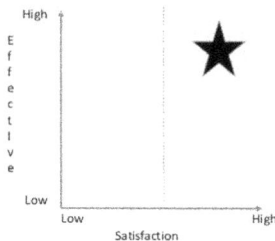

Figure 21: Effectiveness - Satisfaction Matrix

Piloting the Change

Having developed an organisational perspective on the functionality of the revised product or service, developing a **prototype to test** whether the improved version is adequately valued by customers is a prudent step. Even quite small changes in your product / services or the supporting processes benefit from being evaluated. As Behavioural Economist Richard Thaler (2015) points out, in addition to a change itself, an equally important innovation can be the **insistence that all interventions are tested** using a robust methodology such as the sort of randomized control trials (RCT) used in medical research. In his book, *"Misbehaving: The Making of Behavioural Economics",* he explains the use of RCT to evaluate different versions of a letter from the UK Tax Collection Authority, intended to improve collection rates by applying Behavioural Economics (Nudge) concepts. In this case people were assigned at random to receive differently worded letters (including a control group that received the original wording).

Whatever the proposed product or service change, a rapid prototyping and testing of the ideas should provide you with additional information that will help increase the **probability of success** and reduce the **risk of over-complicating** the offering.

Balancing efficiency and innovation

As enterprises strive to improve the quality of the services and products that they supply today, inevitable tensions will arise with the work necessary to develop new opportunities. Shona Brown and Kathleen Eisenhardt (1996) in their book "*Product Innovation As Core Capability: The Art of Continuous Change*" highlight that innovative organisations operate on the edge of chaos. They continually have to **balance the operational needs** of satisfying todays customers and their workforce, **with the future needs** of their enterprise. A challenge for leaders is to legitimise both the delivery and improvement of current offerings and the time and expense necessary to develop the next generation of enterprise offerings. Some, such as Tushman & O'Reilly (1996) describe this as **Organisational ambidexterity**.

Please activate the QR code below (or type http://wp.me/P3ep12-sY into your browser) to reach a web page containing a number of templates and useful links to further information.

3 RAISING AGILITY

"In turbulent markets, organizational agility, which I define as the capacity to identify and capture opportunities more quickly than rivals do, is invaluable. Executives know this: a recent McKinsey survey found that nine out of ten executives ranked organizational agility both as critical to business success and as growing in importance over time. The benefits of enhanced agility, according to survey respondents, include higher revenues, more satisfied customers and employees, improved operational efficiency, and a faster time to market."

McKinsey Quarterly, *Competing through Organizational Agility*
http://www.mckinsey.com/insights/managing_in_uncertainty/competing_thro
ugh_organizational_agility

The *2014 Forbes Insights Study "Making the Change – Planning, Executing and Measuring Successful Business Transformation"* highlights failure to anticipate market changes as the biggest challenge to successful business transformation initiatives.[23] The primary purpose of this chapter is to inspire broader thinking about the future of your enterprise.

"Because companies are usually divided into organizational silos, the information leaders need to see and assess an approaching threat is often fragmented. Various people have various pieces of the puzzle, but no one has them all. In theory, corporate management should play the role of synthesizer, bringing together the fragmented information in order to see the big picture. But the barriers to this happening are great. Information is filtered as it moves up through hierarchies – sensitive or embarrassing information is withheld or glossed over."[24]

This chapter is intended as a platform for raising the strategic agility of your organisation. Some of the frameworks and tools discussed have been foundations for the extensive work done by Corporate Planning departments in the past. My objective is not to persuade you to allocate resources to huge annual planning efforts but rather to **use the frameworks to continuously develop insights on changes** in your marketplace. For example, when people started spending more on Smartphones and mobile phone charges, was there a correlation with less spending on other leisure activities? Perhaps the

---

[23] Forbes, *Forbes Insights Study - Making the Change – Planning, Executing and Measuring Successful Business Transformation*, Forbes, 2014.

[24] Watkins, M.D., Bazerman, M.H., *Predictable Surprises – The Disasters that you should have seen coming*, Harvard Business Review, March 2003.

amount of socialising in bars and pubs or the volume of gym memberships would fall as people needed to make economies in order to pay for their Smartphones? Was the virtual networking available through the Smartphone a substitute for meeting people in pubs and fitness clubs? If you own a fitness club, and are armed with this insight, can you develop services that turn the Smartphone into something that **augments** your fitness club **rather than becomes a substitute** for membership?

Effective strategic thinking has a **laser like beam**. It penetrates all the way from an enterprise's purpose, through to initiatives that grow enterprise capabilities (with measures and targets), to address the needs of customers, consumers, employees and other stakeholders. As you think about this, a good discipline is to look through **the lens** of a **spectrum of the customers**, and then the "lenses" of other stakeholders:

- What does success look like for each of these groups?
- What developments are there in the market place that may influence these views?

The first part of this chapter is designed to help you develop a **broader understanding** of your market. Opportunities to innovate or capture market share will then be more apparent, as your capability to anticipate and sense changes, increases. Subsequently I will discuss how enterprises can develop more efficient, effective and consistent reflexes, to **exploit** these **opportunities**.

How agile is your Enterprise?

The following 12 questions were posed in an Accenture *Outlook Journal* article[25]. Please answer the questions as a start point for thinking further about business agility in your enterprise.

1.	Does your organisation have at least three scenarios for how your industry is most likely to evolve over the next 36 months? Does it have good options for responding?
2.	What three big opportunities would your company be pursuing if it were more agile?
3.	Imagine three possible sources of competition that you haven't thought about until now. How will you respond to them?
4.	Put yourself in your top competitors' shoes. What could they do to disrupt the market in the next year, and what are your plans for outsmarting them?
5.	How is your company augmenting its ability to quickly sense new market anomalies? Are you taking full advantage of the new capabilities of today's analytics tools?
6.	What are the three biggest factors preventing your organisation from becoming more agile? How do you plan to overcome them?
7.	Did you make such big cuts during the recession (particularly in terms of talent) that your agility and ability to grow have been damaged? If so, how are you compensating now for those cuts?
8.	In what areas should you be collaborating with competitors to drive changes in the market?
9.	Who among your organization's new leaders will be most effective at taking advantage of volatility? What makes them different from your long-time leaders?
10.	Which of your competitors are the best leading indicators of future

---

[25] Shill, W., Engel, J.F., Mann, D., Schatteman, O., Corporate Agility: Six ways to make volatility your friend, Accenture Outlook Journal, No 3, 2012.

> market opportunities?
> 11. Where would faster decision-making be of most benefit to your company?
> 12. Have you been able to cut your company's fixed costs in the past few years to improve its agility?

The spectrum of **frameworks, tools and techniques** in this book are intended to help YOU develop actions to **address** any areas of **weakness** that you identified in your answers to this questionnaire.

Assessing the "As Is" of your Enterprise

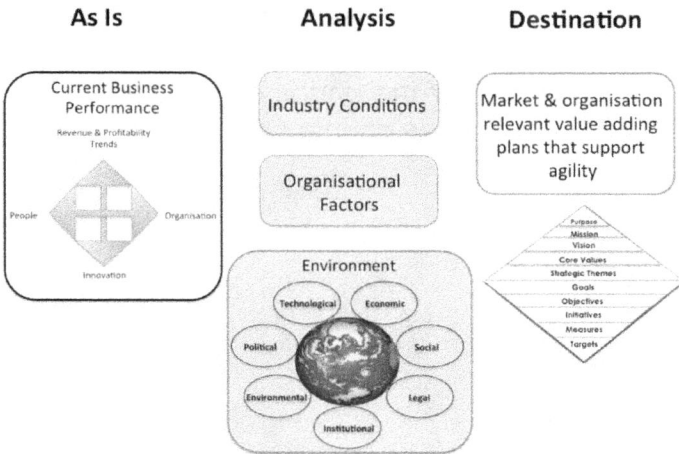

Figure 22: The Agility Journey

The start point for our journey is an assessment of your **current business performance**. We will then consider industry conditions and broader issues in your competitive environment. This broader understanding will enable **YOU** to **anticipate, sense, respond** and **adapt** to the changing business conditions. This Strategic agility is the **destination** for this climb towards more sustainable performance.

Current Financial Performance

How profitable is your enterprise? In general the financial performance of enterprises follows an "S" curve as revenues grow slowly at first and then faster as the enterprise's products or services are more widely adopted. At some point the market matures, competition increases and revenue growth slows. Then as substitute products or services appear, or the underlying customer need disappears, revenues go into decline.

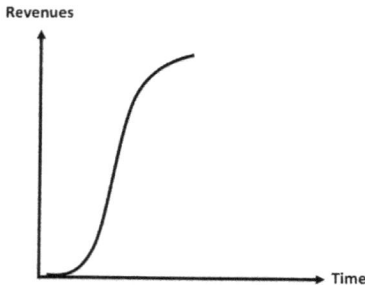

Figure 23: The Revenue "S Curve"

If the growth rate of your **revenues is slowing, ask why**? Perhaps the market for your product /

service is now saturated? Is there a new competitor? Have the prices, or the positioning of your products in relation to those of your competitors changed? Are you entering what I term a **Nokia-Sony-Blackberry phase** where a fundamentally new product / service (in these cases the Smartphone) is becoming more popular with buyers than the product / service that you are offering? Have there been **changes within your enterprise** that are negatively impacting growth? Have changes in your sales force subdued growth?

The **Sales Force** can be a great **source of market intelligence** if engaged positively. As Bernard Lunn, a seasoned Information Systems Entrepreneur, points out, if sales are falling:

"The first instinct is to "give the sales team a sharp kick in the pants". That may be all that is needed. Or it may be that the sales team is acting like the canary in the coal mine that is alerting you to a shift in the market that you have to address at a more strategic level; disruption can sneak up on you."[26]

If the sales team is forecasting a drop in sales **do you understand why**? Moreover, how accurate are the sales forecasts? If **forecast accuracy is suddenly dropping**, this could be an early **sign of disruption** in your market place.

---

[26] Lunn, B., *Mindshare to Marketshare*, Amazon, 2014.

On the hand, if you are on the growth part of the S curve, great. However, it is prudent to keep in mind an observation made by the late Andy Grove, the former CEO of Intel (who navigated that company from making memory chips to microprocessors):

"Business success contains the seeds of its own destruction. Success breeds complacency. Complacency breeds failure. Only the paranoid survive." [27]

Turning to **profitability**, are you in the ranges of "A", "B" or "C" in the graphic below? Are your strategies and tactics consistent with the actions needed to improve the business from these positions? If you are in the "C" zone, do you understand why?

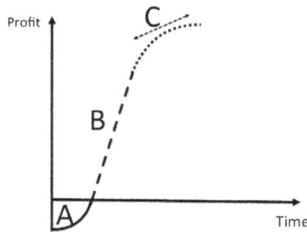

Figure 24: The Profit "S curve"

For example, is you productivity[28] static? In may enterprises, productivity improves in the early

---

[27] Grove, A.S., *Only the Paranoid Survive: How to Exploit the Crisis Points that Challenge Every Company and Career.* Broadway Business, 1996.

years as growth provides economies of scale. Later however productivity flat-lines. Consider:

Your Annual Revenues
The Annual Hours worked by your staff and contractors

Can you relate the productivity of your organisation to either of the following 2 graphs?

---

[28] If you are not an Economist or particularly analytical you might find it helpful to think of productivity as defined by Charles Duhigg (2016): "Productivity is the name we give our attempts to figure out the best uses of our energy, intellect and time as we try to seize the most meaningful rewards with the least wasted effort".

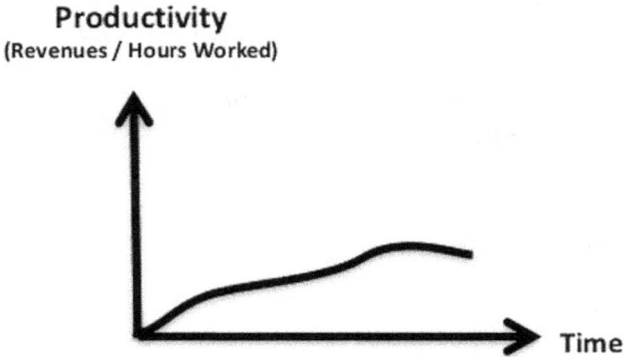

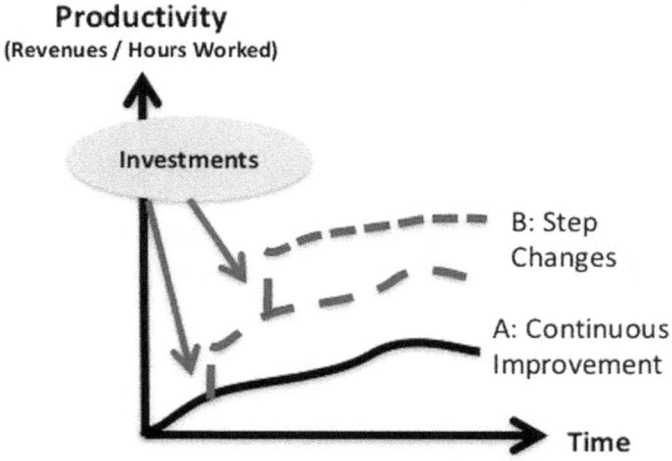

Figure 25: Productivity trends

If your revenues are slowing, for whatever reason, what is happening to the level of company debt? Increasing (or even static) debt, when revenues growth is slowing (consider the previous revenue S curve discussion) can be an early warning sign of financial stress.

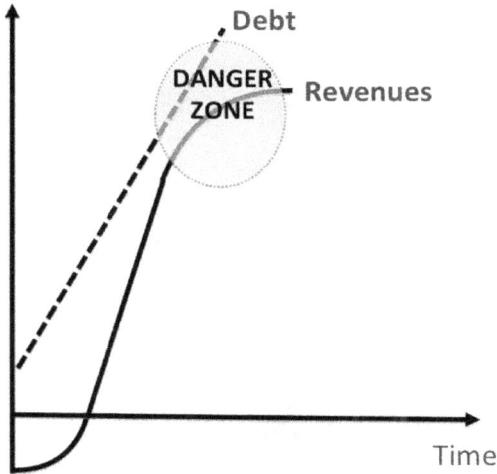

Figure 26: The Revenue - Debt Danger Zone

If your business in this **Danger Zone**, I urge you to commission an urgent, holistic, state of the business review. As John Ashcroft states, know your burn rate, and "Make sure you take off before the cash runs out!"[29]

Is your **profitability** providing an **adequate return** on the capital invested in your enterprise? Are you meeting the growth and profitability

---

[29] http://www.slideshare.net/jkaonline/strategy-guidelines-from-the-dimensions-of-strategy-team?utm_source=slideshow&utm_medium=ssemail&utm_campaign=post_upload_view_cta

expectations of your key stakeholders? Do you include the cost of capital when considering profitability?

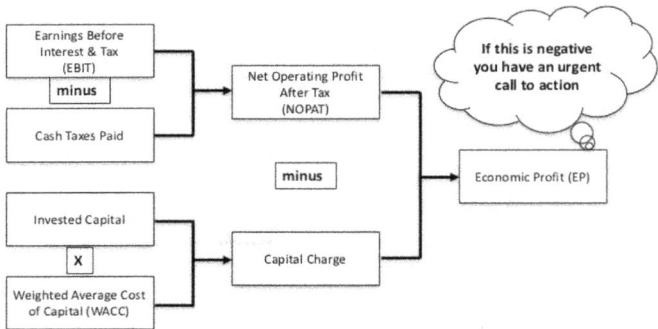

Figure 27: Are you making a positive economic profit?

As you read through this book, use the tools and frameworks to **generate questions** and potential explanations for where your enterprise is on your financial "S curves". More importantly, **anticipate** where you are going to be in one, two and three years' time. Use this understanding to proactively develop tactics to optimize your enterprise performance.

The same "S curve" thinking can provide insights into how the **distinctiveness** of your **capabilities** is **evolving**.

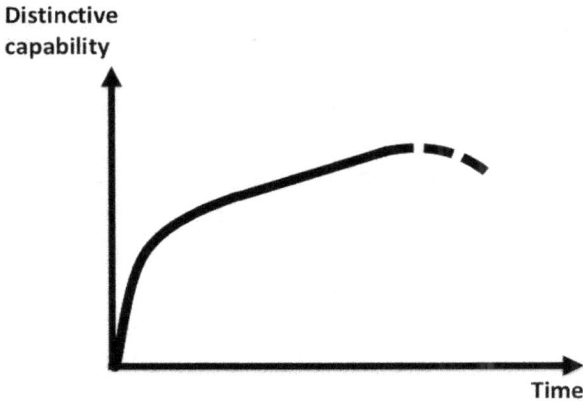

Figure 28: Distinctive Capability "S curve"

As you develop a **novel idea** and build capabilities around it, the distinctiveness of your capabilities grows. Unless you have strong intellectual property protection, it is likely that your commercial success will act as a magnet. Others will come into your market place and erode your distinctive position. Their products or services may meet the same customer or similar customer needs at lower prices or in different ways. Unless you are able to innovate and **continuously bring new value** byadding features to your product or service, it is likely that the distinctiveness of your capabilities will decline. This can be a leading indicator of a slow-down in revenue growth (or at least profitability). Developing a sense of the rate at which the performance of a product can continue to improve - its **performance trajectory** - can help you forecast the future trend of your revenues from the product / service concerned.

For example, in the early days of cloud services in the information systems arena, enterprises could develop **distinctive positions** in the new marketplace and grow quickly. Then larger enterprises such as Amazon, Microsoft and Oracle, entered the market. The small enterprises that continued to innovate could extend the period where their **distinctive capability** was a competitive advantage over the large global information systems enterprises.

Your Market Place

A range of **local and global forces** is pounding the markets for our products and services. In the past, many industries had the luxury of time to adjust to these market forces. These forces are NOW creating ever **more rapid changes** in our **competitive environment**. We need to sense and respond quickly so that we continue to grow our revenues and profits.

"we compete against market transitions, not competitors. Product transitions used to take five to seven years; now they take one or two."
John Chambers the CEO of CISCO[30]

This section is intended to help you **improve your understanding** of the forces acting on YOUR marketplace and help you to **ask the RIGHT questions**. The foundation is my belief that we can all **use strategic analysis to expand our thinking**. Doing this will reduce the temptation to restrict our planning to threats and opportunities that **we already know**!

Andrew Pettigrew, a Strategy Professor with an anthropological background, studied the politics of strategic decision[31] some years ago. He was fascinated by the inertial properties of organisations. He showed that organisations frequently hold on to **faulty assumptions about their world.** He identified a number of examples where there was overwhelming evidence that an organisation's world had changed and, moreover, that they should change too. In our rapidly changing world, **sensing necessary changes earlier** than competitors is a **foundation** for the **nimbleness** organisations need. Enterprises that can embed an **ability to move quickly** into their corporate DNA, have a basis for **creating more value** for their stakeholders.

---

[30] Schumpeter Column in The Economist, 19 March 2016:
http://www.economist.com/news/business-and-finance/21694962-managing-them-hard-businesses-are-embracing-idea-working-teams
[31] Pettigrew, Andrew M, *The Politics of organizational decision-making*, 1973.

The more I have seen of traditional SWOT (Strengths, Weaknesses, Opportunities and Threats) analysis (even when turned around to TOWS to focus on the external factors first), the less value I have sensed in the exercise. Fortunately there is another well-established approach. Drawing on Industrial Organisation theory from Economics, Michael Porter of the Harvard Business School developed a 5-force framework that considered the supply-side of the economics of a business, to **assess the competitive intensity of a market**. The underlying assumption is that **the more intense the competition**, the **less profitable** a market will be. The Porter 5-force framework considers:

a. Three "horizontal" influences – the **threat of new entrants** to the market, the **threat of substitute products** and the **competitive rivalry** amongst the enterprises competing in a given market. New and evolving technologies increase the probability of new entrants and substitute products arriving in your market place **from potentially unexpected sources**. For example, will developments in software-defined networks be a foundation for Amazon or Google to compete with established telecoms networks? If your products and services provide more sophisticated capabilities than your customers use, you may be at a particular risk of new entrants offering simple **basic** offerings at materially lower cost[32]. As these new **disruptive** entrants to the market gain in experience and scale, they may well develop more **cutting edge** products and services, that are a threat to all the established enterprises in the particular market place. Smartphones are an example. The early phones offered as niche products (with limited performance) were not a substitute for personal computers. After a few years, the market went into an explosive growth period, after the launch of the Apple and Android Smartphones. Now, many people access the internet using a Smartphone rather than a Personal Computer.

b. Two "vertical" influences – the **power of buyers** of your product / service and the **power of sellers** of the inputs you need to produce your product or service. For example, if one company purchases the bulk of your products, your buyers have a potentially worrying degree of power as some suppliers to large retailers have found out (just before their business ceased to exist). In the original Porter 5 forces

---

[32] Clayton Christensen (2016) observed that "Disruptive innovations create an entirely new market through the introduction of a new kind of product or service, one that's actually worse, initially, as judged by the performance metrics that mainstream customers value."

framework Buyers and Sellers were considered as a potential drain on profitability and strategic actions to limit their power were encouraged.

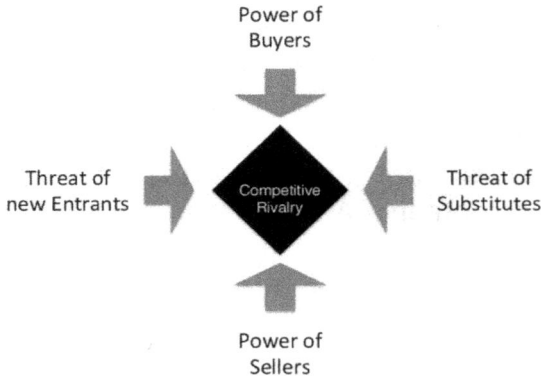

Figure 29: Porter 5 Forces

In the November 2014 *Harvard Business Review*, Michael Porter demonstrated the effectiveness of this long established framework in analysing the markets for "Smart Connected Products". This provided evidence that the tool remains an effective way of developing insights[33] on developing and maintaining competitive power, through combating the five forces.

---

[33] Porter, M.E., Heppelman, J.E., *How Smart, Connected Products Are Transforming Competition*, Harvard Business Review, November 2014.

After Porter's original work the late Andy Grove, the former CEO of Intel, argued that the **power of complementary products** should also be considered. For example, when Microsoft stopped supporting Windows XP, companies had an additional incentive to upgrade to newer versions of the Windows operating system and in many cases this necessitated purchasing new Personal Computers – increasing the demand for Intel chips etc. Shopping centres are another example of an enterprise gaining from customers being able to benefit from other products and services while purchasing / consuming yours.

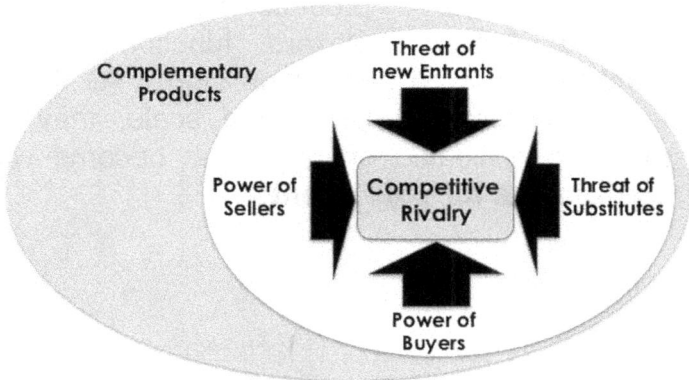

Figure 30: Porter 5 Forces + Complementary Products

In recent years this thinking has been extended further to include **Network effects** that flow from being part of a community that can enhance the value obtained from using your product or service. The applications stores developed for the Apple and Android Smartphones, for example, provided material competitive advantages over the more restricted offering that were being provided by the likes of Blackberry. Whilst the original Porter 5 Forces focused on the Supply-Side drivers, in our internet economy demand side economies of scale develop as networks expand and where **effective platforms emerge.** Where these effectively match material numbers of sellers and buyers of services, new forms of competition can emerge quickly. As Clayton Christensen (2016) has pointed out, new **disruptive** entrants to a market may initially offer different, and generally inferior service / product characteristics (for example limited software functionality in a purchase from an application store). As the new entrant gains experience and scale, they offer more sophisticated offerings that become viable **alternatives for your clients**.

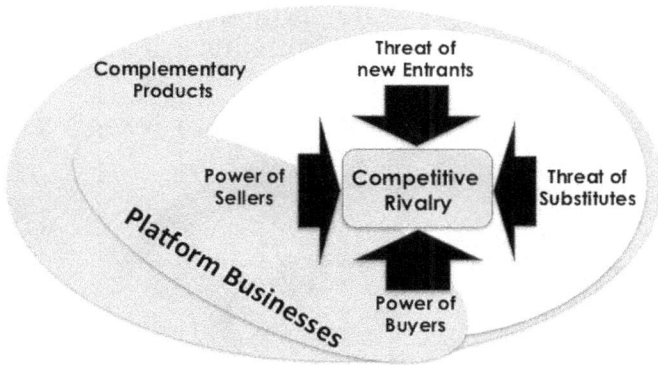

Figure 31: Porter 5 Forces + Platform Businesses

Subsequently others have suggested that the Porter framework should also recognize the influence of **governments** and **regulation**. When the US government deregulated the road transport industry and opened up the opportunity for entrepreneurs to create the modern courier companies, opportunities to improve the efficiency and effectiveness of existing industry supply chains mushroomed. Moreover the infrastructure that was created provided a critical foundation for Amazon etc. Looking to the future, if for example, regulators simplify the process and requirements for banking licenses, the **Threat of New Entrants** to the Banking market is likely to rise. This is being seen in the United Kingdom as this book is being written. On the other hand, Aereo, the New York based start-up that enabled streaming of High Definition TV programmes to Smartphones, Laptops and Tablets etc. was overcome by the weight of legal and regulatory barriers after lobbying from media incumbents in 2014[34].

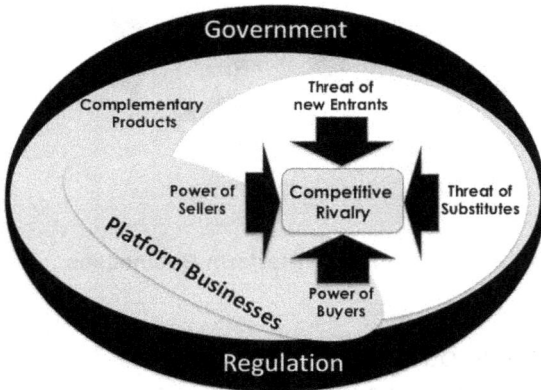

Figure 32: Porter 5 Forces + 2

Changes in your political, economic, legal, social, technological, ecological and institutional environment.

"I skate to where the puck is going, not where it has been."

Wayne Gretzky [35]

[34] The Financial Times, *Disrupters bring Disruption and Opportunity*, 28 December 2014. http://www.ft.com/cms/s/2/b9677026-8b6d-11e4-ae73-00144feabdc0.html#slide0

[35] Quoted by Alastair Campbell in *Winners and How they Succeed*, Hutchinson, Randon House, 2015.

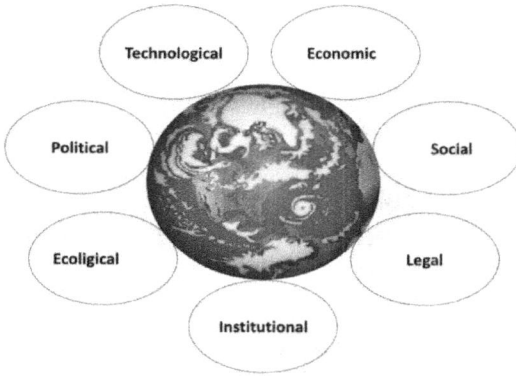

Figure 33: Environmental Analysis

A good first step is a brainstorming session. The focus should be to consider **how** factors in the **political, economic, legal, social, technological, ecological and institutional environment** (PESTELI) will impact your enterprise in the next 3 years. If you include a broad spectrum of experience, this brainstorming can provide invaluable insights into how these external forces may evolve. It can be helpful to start by including an example of an external event that a company should have predicted. For example the attack by Greenpeace activists on Shell's Brent Spar Oil Storage platform in the North Sea in 1995, after the company had announced that it planned to sink the structure:

"The attack on the Spar had clearly come as a surprise to the company. But should it have? Shell actually had all the information it needed to predict what would transpire. The company's own security advisers entertained the possibility that environmental activists might try to block the dumping." [36]

Following the initial brainstorming, a discussion of probabilities[37] of each potential issue can help focus further thinking.

After an initial dialogue amongst your executive colleagues, a **broader input** from a spectrum of your **staff** would be valuable – perhaps using "themes" identified by the Executives to provoke thinking. In the Building Stakeholder Engagement" chapter, I explain the "Excellence Audit^{TM}" from the Tom Peters Company as a tool for securing such staff involvement.

Ideally, the discussion is then extended to include **perspectives** from your **suppliers, alliance partners** and **customers,** covering the full

---

[36] Watkins, M.D., Bazerman, M.H., *Predictable Surprises – The Disasters that you should have seen coming*, Harvard Business Review, March 2003.

[37] In his book *Smarter faster better*, Charles Duhigg argues that developing predictions and influencing probabilities improves decision making. "The people who make the best choices are the ones who work hardest to envision various futures, to write them down and think them through, and then ask themselves, which ones do I think are most likely and why? Anyone can learn to make better decisions. We can all train ourselves to see small predictions we make every day. But with practice, we can learn how to influence the probability that our fortune-telling comes true." This is a theme I will return to later in this book in the discussion of scenario planning.

spectrum of factors influencing your business environment.

For example, the growing **impact of social media** can have quite profound impacts on enterprises. I recall an enterprise where any form of external communication required clearance by a raft of individuals across the corporate functions. This included frequently slow reviews by legal and brand departments. The time taken to do this would extend to many days if not weeks. Contrast this with the expectations of customers using Twitter. The **moment of value**, for an enterprise quoted in a Tweet to engage in dialogue, is perhaps one hour at most. What does this mean for delegating, empowering, developing and **trusting** junior staff to respond to tweets? What training do you need to provide? What does it mean for the people you recruit?

The constant **innovation** facilitated by technological advances is a broader cause of faster response time. In their book "*Big Bang Disruption: Business Survival in the Age of Constant Innovation*", Larry Downes and Paul Nunes included a question and answer from Ernest Hemingway's book "*The Sun Also Rises*". **"How did you go bankrupt?"** "**Two ways. Gradually and then suddenly.**"

> *"One of the most consistent patterns in business is the failure of leading companies to stay at the top of their industries when technologies or markets change"*
>
> Clayton Christensen (2016)

Enduring enterprises have a knack for keeping close to their customers so that they understand how to prioritise investments on new technology that clients will buy, while also sensing emerging technologies that may in future be critical for their survival[38]. They also successfully strike the balance between profitably meeting current needs and shrewd investments that keep their competencies **cutting edge**. By doing this, they limit the space for new entrants with new technology to gain a foothold in their market places.

I hope that our discussion earlier of S curves has sensitized you to the value of identifying forces that are slowly impacting the **performance** of your business. If you sense that your performance is slowly declining, the time for proactive action is **NOW**. In certain cases, particularly where there is great **technological innovation**, enterprises can be vulnerable to rapid

---

[38] Researchers such as Christensen (2016) have emphasised the importance of thinking beyond the technology needs customers are expressing "...companies listened to their customers, gave them the product performance they were looking for and in the end were hurt by the very technologies their customers led them to ignore...... The very processes that successful, well-managed companies use to serve the rapidly growing needs of their current customers can leave them highly vulnerable when market-changing technologies appear."

destruction by new entrants. For example, manufacturers of public telephone boxes when mobile telephones became affordable. On the other hand, the rapid expansion of Broadband internet services has created new opportunities for a broad spectrum of companies, including those who make the equipment boxes that are now alongside most of our roads in residential areas.

New regulations can potentially have a similarly rapid impact. If the European Union (EU) enacts legislation that requires all corporate data originated in the EU to be maintained on servers in the EU, what would be the impact on public Cloud IT offerings from the likes of Amazon, Google, Microsoft and Oracle, built on global networks?

Turning now to an example in a much more traditional industry. In 2014, the Mackerel industry in Scotland was subjected to **two shocks** that necessitated **immediate action.** Firstly, as a result of conservation measures over many years, the **supply** of Mackerel was increasing significantly. This supply-side shock, created concern that prices would drop. Secondly, a political action **undermined demand** when the Russian Government retaliated to sanctions introduced by the West (following instability in the Ukraine) by banning food imports from the European Union[39].

---

[39] BBC Radio, *Peter Day's World of Business*, 27 November 2014.

Enterprises in the Mackerel industry needed to invest fast in major business development initiatives to find new markets to take the supplies traditionally bought by Russia.

Moving on to Institutions, Niall Ferguson, the Historian and presenter of TV series such as The House of Rothschild, argues that we should not assume the effectiveness of representative government, the free market or the rule of law and civil society.

"The fact is in today's climate there seems to be a real lack of faith in institutions - all over the world ..." [40]

Sridharan Nair, Managing Partner, PwC Malaysia

Enterprises are likely to operate increasingly across market places with very **different levels of institutional maturity**. Moreover, enterprises that are reliant on **new business models** that rely on platforms to link buyers and sellers rely on the effective governance of the platform concerned.

"Platform executives must make smart choices about access (whom to let onto the platform) and governance (or "control" – what consumers, producers, providers and even competitors are allowed to do there)." [41]

---

[40] Nair, S, *3 ways to build trust in your business,* World Economic Forum, 30 May 2016. Available from https://www.weforum.org/agenda/2016/05/3-ways-to-build-trust-in-your-business-05866831-1d47-4d4f-8b16-88ad8e0b7e59/

[41] Van Alstyne, M.W., Parker, G.G., Choudary, S.P., *Pipelines, Platforms, and the New Rules of Strategy*, Harvard Business Review, April 2016.

These new institutions include more involvement from a broader spectrum of stakeholders – for example, participants can provide open feedback about buyers and sellers on the platform. Whilst there is evidence that on some platforms this feedback has been manipulated inappropriately, platforms such as Amazon and eBay etc. have demonstrated that they can continuous refine their governance arrangements as the platform matures. I sense two trends that all enterprises should address:

- an appetite amongst consumers for greater transparency,
- individuals' readiness to give more weight to the opinions of peers than authority.

Niall Ferguson suggests[42] that even in countries with well-established traditional institutions, the effectiveness of these institutions is degenerating.

"....narrowly economic explanations that focus on financial forces ('deleveraging'), international integration ('globalization'), the role of information technology ('offshoring' and 'outsourcing') or fiscal policy ('stimulus' versus 'austerity') do not offer sufficient explanation.

---

[42] Ferguson, N., *The Great Degeneration*, Penguin Books, 2013.

We need to delve into the history of institutions to understand the complex dynamics of convergence and divergence that characterize today's world."

Niall Ferguson

Oil exploration companies operating in Northern Iraq, for example, have had repeated challenges as the institutions they need to deal with evolve rapidly – culminating on occasions in a total lack of access to the pipelines they need to export the oil they extract. The impact that such degeneration may have on particular enterprises, in particular countries, may or may not be material; however, I believe that the role and **effectiveness of institutions** is a factor that should be included in any environmental **analysis** used to **inform strategic direction**.

All the Political, Economic, Social, Technological, Legal, Ecological and Institutional (PESTLEI) dimensions can be **drivers of material change** in competitive potential and the underlying economics of **your enterprise**. Increasingly, in our ever more interconnected world, the individual changes in the PESTLEI environment have a broader impact on the eco-system around a business. For example, the technology changes such as 4G mobile telecommunications informing us of our **trusted friends** views on the products and global trends, next generation product introductions elsewhere in the world perhaps, **before** we make our **purchase decisions**.

"the technological revolution is not just changing what we do and how we do it – it is changing us, it is changing our lives, and it is changing the way we see the world."
Klaus Schwab (2015)

Making **proactive** adjustments to your business, and potentially developing new alliances with other enterprises (perhaps to exploit new business platforms such as Smartphone Applications), will improve the likelihood of continuing to achieve your profit and other stakeholder objectives. For example Downes and Nunes (2014) suggest that innovations in pharmaceuticals are becoming rarer because the increasing cost of regulation has **changed the economics** of the business (as the period of patent protection from generic drugs is not expected to offer sufficient financial returns). Provided that Anti-Trust issues can be overcome, this may open up innovation in the way drug company R&D is funded and ignite a new wave of development. For example, Robert Litan envisages pooling the R&D expenses of a spectrum of enterprises and packaging these as securities:

"Structured the right way, pharma R&D bonds could be not only attractive for investors but also a potentially important way to bring more capital to support research for drug

therapies and medical devices that both extend and improve the quality of life for millions of people."

Robert Litan[43]

Harnessing "Big Data" and Business Intelligence / Analytics

"80% of the World's data has been created in the last 24 months"

Rich Clayton Vice-President Analytics, Oracle

"Every two days now we create as much information as we did from the dawn of civilization up until 2003"

Eric Schmidt, Google

The growing **volume of business data** is creating a huge opportunity to understand both our markets and our own enterprises better. Consider the mass of social media data, all the transactions we undertake electronically, the sites we visit on the Internet, our locations as we use our Smartphones and the increasing numbers of devices directly connected to each other over the Internet. Some observers such as Paul O'Riordan, Oracle's Head of Business Analytics for the UK and Ireland, argue that we are now at a tipping point. This is a result of:

---

[43] Litan, R.E., *Economists: Don't leave home without one*, McKinsey Quarterly April 2015

- The widespread availability of tablet computers (that provide a more engaging user experience than traditional Personal Computers),
- The Power of technology (both hardware, that is allowing database utilities to be embedded onto chips, and business analytics software that is easy to use by business - as opposed to IT specialists),
- The ready availability of data – albeit much of it unstructured.

With such a mass of data and analytical tools, an increasing challenge is to **ask the right questions.** In his book *"Big Data – Using SMART Big Data and Metrics to make Better Decisions and Improve Performance"*, Bernard Marr urges a disciplined approach that starts with Strategy.

> *"In order to cut through the chaos, confusion and sheer volume of data that can or does exist we must therefore "Start with Strategy". Instead of starting with data, start with your business objectives and what you are specifically trying to achieve. This will automatically point you toward questions that you need to answer which will immediately narrow data requirements into manageable areas."*

Bernard Marr [44]

---

[44] Marr, B., *Big Data – Using Smart Big Data Analytics and metrics to make better decisions and improve performance*, Willey, 2015, , page 20.

As data from multiple sources is combined, the **potential value can increase dramatically**; however, only if appropriate data analytics is applied. The tools I have explained earlier in this chapter provide a **foundation for developing questions** that can start a process that focuses the data analytics efforts so that you gain actionable insights from the data collected. In the words of Robert Litan, *"Data mining is likely to be more useful if guided by underlying theories"*[45]. These insights should raise the level of agility of your enterprise and help you make **better decisions**.

For example a mobile telephone company's **5-Force analysis** may have identified the likelihood of increasing competition as a new entrant joins your market. On the basis of your experience, you believe that it is easier to retain an existing customer than to attract a new one. You therefore decide to seek to understand more about the customers that have cancelled their contracts over the last six months. You commission analysis to establish whether there are any **patterns** amongst the customers that have left. This analysis highlights a significant number of customers who use an average of between 600 and 750 MB of data a month are leaving. These customers are

---

[45] Litan, R.E., *Economists: Don't leave home without one,* McKinsey Quarterly April 2015

only light users of the calls and texts that historically was the backbone of your enterprise. Analysis of your competitors' monthly contract options shows that one has a new monthly plan that includes 750 MB of data but low call and text allowances. The monthly subscription is only 60% of your charges. Armed with this analysis, and your knowledge of your new spare data capacity, you decide to offer an additional option. This will include 750 MB of data but less calls and texts. As the **targets** for this new offering appear to use email more than texts or voice calls, you decide to email these customers when they reach the 11-month point of their 12-month contracts. When you go to thank the person who did the analysis for you, she demonstrates a **Business Analytics** software tool. It is really easy to use, with lots of **drag and drop** options and no requirement to write code. You decide that the tool should be built into an iPad Application (**with appropriate security controls** to safeguard corporate data) and then distributed to all members of your Leadership Team.

Using Data to Manage People Better

Where the necessary data is captured, **Data Analytics tools** can be used to help **match** individual's skills, capabilities, availability and aspirations with vacant roles, tasks and initiatives. Enterprises with an easily searchable database of information about their people can provide leaders with **timely insights** on the interests and capabilities of their people. Leaders are then equipped to make **better decisions** and nudge people in a direction that creates added value for **both the individual and the enterprise**. Siemens, for example, invests in maintaining such a database. This is a foundation for developing their people and matching them to the **tasks needed** to realise the Siemens vision[46]. Google analysed a broad spectrum of data in a quest to understand whether managers added value in the very technical Google context.[47]

In addition to improving decision making, data that is well managed can provide leaders with the confidence to move away from the sort of 20th Century centralized command and control approaches that constrains agile performance.

---

[46] The Times 100 Business Case Studies, "Creating a high performance culture - A Siemens case study"
http://businesscasestudies.co.uk/siemens/creating-a-high-performance-culture/talent-management.html#axzz2tIteOnzc

[47] The research concluded that at Google great managers add value by:
- being good coaches,
- empowering their team and not micromanaging,
- expressing interest / concern for team members' success and personal wellbeing,
- being productive and results orientated,
- being a good communicator (listening and sharing information),
- helping with career development,
- having a clear vision/strategy for the team
- having important technical skills that help him/her advise the team.

Holding accurate and relevant people data, speeds **planning**, speeds **business decisions** and enables leaders to **identify problem areas earlier.**[48]

7-S Analysis

"The CEO's role is to harness the social forces in the organisation, to shape and guide values ...... good value-shapers are effective managers (in contrast with mere manipulators of formal rewards who deal only with the narrower concept of efficiency)"

Chester Barnard [49]

Another well-established framework that is helpful in thinking about both an enterprise **As Is** and business improvement actions is the **7-S**. Tom Peters, Rob Waterman, Julian Phillips and Anthony Athos developed the framework in the 1980s. The project that created the framework included primary research, conducted at a broad spectrum of enterprises and academic institutions, and consideration of established management literature. The assertion at the top of this section harks back to the earlier days of management research and was highlighted when the framework was originally published[50]. I believe that it

---

[48] Marr, B., *Big Data – Using Smart Big Data Analytics and metrics to make better decisions and improve performance*, Willey, 2015 page 50.

[49] Barnard, Chester Irving, *The functions of the executive*, 1938.

resonates even more powerfully today, in our world of social media.

The **7-S framework** was a key component of "*In Search of Excellence*" – the classic management book subsequently authored by Tom Peters and Rob Waterman[51].

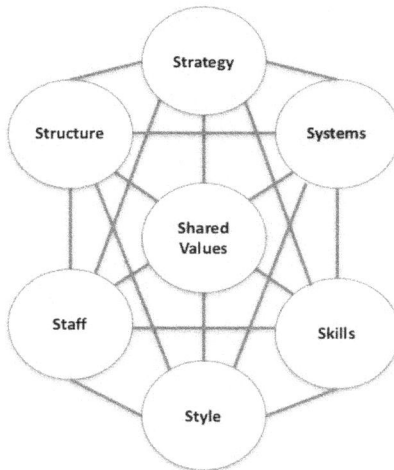

Figure 34: 7S Analysis

The underlying thinking emphasises that effective enterprises are a consequence of more than purely great strategy and appropriate structure. For example, an enterprise with strong

---

[50] Peters. T, Phillips, J. Waterman. R, *Structure is not Organization*, Business Horizons, June 1980.

[51] Peters, Tom & Waterman, Robert, *In Search of Excellence*, 1982.

shared-values, in its DNA, can be expected to make effective decisions at more junior levels. This reduces **the burden** on the senior leaders, whose capacity to process the increasing volume of information available in most enterprises, is a limitation. This challenge is ever more apparent in our agile world, where **Big Data** has the potential to provide **more insights,** and our volatile marketplaces necessitate **faster responses**. Fundamental to understanding and applying the **7 S**, is an appreciation of both the **variables** and the **interconnections**. An effective programme of actions to improve organisational effectiveness will address both. Tom Peters has emphasised that the "real energy required to re-direct an institution comes when all the variables in the model are aligned."

"I continue to say, over 30 years later, that the power of the 7-Ss and In Search of Excellence (1982) and my subsequent work can best be captured in six words: "Hard is soft. Soft is hard." That is, it's the plans and the numbers that are often "soft" (e.g., the sky-high soundness scores that the ratings agencies gave packages of dubious mortgages). And the people ("staff") and shared values ("corporate culture") and skills ("core competencies" these days) which are truly "hard"—that is, the bedrock upon which the adaptive and enduring enterprise is built. To state the obvious, we very much included the "Hard Ss" (Strategy, Structure, Systems) in our framework, then added the "Soft Ss" (Style, Staff, Skills, Shared values—or Superordinate goal); and insisted that there was no precedence among them. Deal with all seven or accept the consequences - likely less than effective

implementation of any project or program or increase in overall organization performance."

Tom Peters[52]

The current Tom Peters **Future Shape of the Winner** framework takes this a stage further by using a Gyroscope as a metaphor. This reflects the essential requirement of maintaining alignment, as the overall enterprise moves at **increasing speed** in our **agile world**. This will be discussed further in the next chapter.

Before examining each of the 7-S variables in turn, I should stress that there is **no hierarchy** amongst the 7 variables and they have no specific order. The driving force amongst the variables, if any, is likely to be specific to a particular enterprise and its current context.

Shared Values (Superordinate Goals)

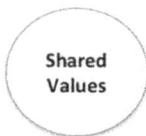

Shared
Values

"…the standards by which employees set priorities that enable them to judge whether an order is attractive or unattractive, whether a customer is more important or less important, whether an idea for a new product is attractive or marginal, and

---

[52] Peters, T., *A Brief History of the 7S [Mckinsey 7-S] Model,* http://tompeters.com/2011/03/a-brief-history-of-the-7-s-mckinsey-7-s-model/, 2011

so on. Prioritisation ideas are made at every level." [53]

Values represent the **core priorities** in an organisation's culture. They drive priorities and shape how individuals act in the organisation. I have consequently elected to start my description of the 7-S factors with the **shared-values** (or superordinate goals as they were originally described). For example, in the case of Disney **guest perception** is the principal Shared Value.

An enterprise's set of values and aspirations (often unwritten) are the fundamental ideas upon which the organisation is built. They include an idea of **future strategic direction** that top management believe should form part of the enterprise DNA. This will include **hard values** such as the **profit margin** expected from products as well as "softer" values that could be considered as **the way things are done around here**. In top performing enterprises these Shared Values are communicated concisely, right through the organisation. Most importantly they are communicated in ways that carry a rich meaning for the people involved. Clayton Christensen, the Harvard Business School Professor that popularised the **disruptive innovation** term, suggests that a key operating metric is the degree

---

[53] Christensen, C.M., *The Clayton M. Christensen Reader*, Harvard Business School Publishing Corporation, 2016

that clear consistent values have permeated the organisation.[54]

Reflecting on my 20 years in professional services organisations, I can recall enterprises where such Shared Values / superordinate goals (for example Best People) were really lived and other cases where they were purely marketing slogans.

The entrepreneurs who establish new enterprises are generally driven by a **set of values,** and in the initial stages of development their enterprise reflects these. As enterprises grow, it is **increasingly hard** to ensure that these values are lived by the employees. This makes it harder for Shared Values to guide individuals' behaviour, decision-making, and resource allocation etc. I believe that the larger the organisation, the more important it is for **values to be institutionalised** so that they provide just such guidance. Values are increasingly important when developing strategies and tactics for rapid implementation, because they often drive the intent and direction for enterprise leaders. Furthermore, in our agile world more and **more empowerment** is needed to **junior levels** in organisations and embedded shared values are at ever more of a premium. I believe that consistently **living** these values, **reduces enterprise risk**,

[54] Christensen, C.M., *The Clayton M. Christensen Reader*, Harvard Business School Publishing Corporation, 2016

minimises the need for complex manuals and other policy documents and most importantly increases employee engagement. This is discussed further in the Stakeholder Engagement Chapter.

Moreover, I believe that effective values based leadership is an effective approach to tackling the lack of trust in Leadership that is being spoken about more frequently. The World Economic Forum 2014[55] survey, for example, included "A lack of values in leadership" in the list of top concerns. The Edelman Trust Barometer[56] report headlined a "Crisis of Leadership", showed that less than 50% of business leaders are trusted in 16 of 23 markets surveyed in 2013. **Trust** in Business Leaders ethics and morality **scored very low**. There were very material variances between the score given by individual to organisations and scores given to the leaders of the organisation. I sense that one driver of this change, is the capability that social media provides for citizens to seek opinions of other citizens easily. This both reduces the perceived need for expert advice and develops increased doubts about the opinions expressed by business leaders etc. In her 1 July 2016, Financial Times Magazine Article, Gillian Tett observed that we are placing increasingly

---

[55] http://www.weforum.org/reports/outlook-global-agenda-2014

[56] http://www.edelman.com/insights/intellectual-property/trust-2013/

more trust on our Facebook friends and Twitter feeds than authorities such as institutions or politicians.

"In our everyday lives, we are moving from a system based around vertical axes of trust, where we trust people who seem to have more authority than we do, to one predicated on horizontal axes of trust: we take advice from our peer group".

As part of establishing a collective understanding of an organisation's shared values, it can be helpful for enterprises to develop a **values statement**[57]. This is most effective when the process used **respects the local cultural norms**. For example, in high respect cultures it may be essential to have separate workshops for each level in an organisation. The description of the organisational values of the enterprise is likely to be **riche**r if a spectrum of methods, ranging from highly analytical and rational to highly creative and divergent, is used in the development of the statement. As the values statement evolves, it is important to identify any differences between the organisation's **preferred values** and its **true values** (the values actually reflected by members' behaviours in the organisation). One approach is to **record each preferred value** on a flash card and ask individual employees to "rank" the values

---

[57] For example, the following is part of a values statement for a plastics company: "We are strategically entrepreneurial in the pursuit of excellence, encouraging original thought and its application, and willing to take risks based on sound business judgment."

with 1, 2, or 3 in terms of the **priority** needed by the organisation. (With 3 indicating that the value is very important to the organisation and 1 that it is least important). Then go through the cards again to rank how people **think the values are actually being enacted** in the organisation. (With 3 indicating that the values are fully enacted and 1 indicating that the value is hardly reflected at all. The discrepancies i.e. where a value is highly preferred (ranked with a 3), but hardly enacted (ranked with a 1), can then form the basis for a programme of initiatives to close the gaps.

Once a values statement is agreed it should be **communicated** to all staff and new joiners (in ways that show top **management commitment** to the values). It then becomes a platform for actions to align actual behaviour with preferred behaviours. Moreover it **informs** the decisions on **future strategies and tactics**. During my days at Andersen Consulting, significant effort was put into explaining the organisation's six core values to new joiners and to employees at key milestones in their career development (for example New Manager School). Values were mentioned as a matter of routine in management discussions and in a broad spectrum of internal communications. I sensed that they were institutionalised into the way we did business from the top to the bottom of the organisation. As I reflect, I draw a stark contrast with my memory of values development in a subsequent organisation. There, **marketing**

sponsored a project to develop a values statement. The project drew on the skills of external consultants and included workshops with a broad spectrum of employees. The outputs of the project included an impressive brochure, additional questions on values in annual appraisals and a commitment to probe individual's values during recruitment processes. The Board enthusiastically endorsed the work done however I could not sense real alignment between Board behaviour and the values! Moreover, our highly educated workforce could see the gaps.

Values driven actions

Much has been written about Leaders and Values. One of the new-year blogs in 2014 that particularly resonated with me was from Dr Rick Brickman.[58] He commented that the top reasons people set goals, and don't achieve them, is either that **they haven't clarified values** or that they don't **have a specific enough plan**. Lolly Daskal identified, in her blog, a sense of purpose as one of the seven habits of remarkable innovators[59]. Forming an overt **cascade** from such a **Purpose**, to **Mission** and **Values** and through **vision**, **goals**, **objectives**, to **initiatives**, **measures** and

---

[58] http://www.rickbrinkman.com

[59] http://www.inc.com/lolly-daskal/the-seven-habits-of-successful-innovators.html

targets can be a **foundation for enduring effectiveness**. Graham Kenny's 2014 Harvard Business Review Blog *"Your Company's Purpose Is Not Its Vision, Mission, or Values"*[60] argues that a **purpose statement** is a valuable complement to traditional vision, mission and values statements. It expresses the **organisation's impact on the people** your enterprise is striving to serve. Kenny quotes the example of Kellogg (the food company) "Nourishing families so they can flourish and thrive."[61] Purpose statements linked in this way provide a **sense of direction** for the **discretionary activity** enterprises rely on, for both continuous improvement, and the development of new products and services. Moreover, a clearly thought through purpose, that is embedded in the business realities of the competitive market, provides a **platform for more fluid business plans**.

When working with enterprises I now integrate a purpose statement into a **strategic diamond**. This helps promote a line of sight from purpose through strategic themes to initiatives, measures and targets. I find it particularly helpful to consider the implications of measures and targets being discussed for the elements higher up the diamond.

---

[60] http://blogs.hbr.org/2014/09/your-companys-purpose-is-not-its-vision-mission-or-values/)

[61] http://www.kelloggcompany.com/en_US/our-vision-purpose.html

For example, if using Internal Rate of Return or Return on Capital Employed financial metrics, the implications for innovation need to be considered when setting targets. (Clayton Christensen, the Harvard Business School Professor and author of the "*Innovators Dilemma*", reinforced this point at the 2014 Drucker Symposium in Vienna)[62].

Figure 35: Efficienarta Strategic Diamond

In closing this discussion of values, I should include a "health warning". I am convinced that enterprises that consistently draw on their values to inform their responses to changes in both their external and internal environments have a higher

[62] BBC, "Peter Day's World of Business", 4 December 2014.

probability of long term success. I am also however sensitive to the risk of an institutionalized set of values, **clouding the ability** to sense changes. Therefore, as one applies strategic tools such as Porter Five Force analysis and the 7-S, it is valuable to **check one's thinking** by asking how other enterprises and start-ups would interpret the emerging changes in the competitive environment that you have identified.

Strategy

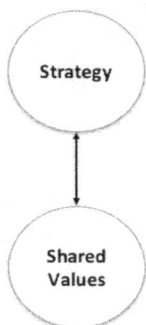

"Strategy is the bit between your purpose and your business plan. People with a clear view of winning know that strategy is everything. You have to have a strategy and stick to it, and never lose the plot."

John Browne (Former CEO of BP)[63]

Alfred Chandler, one of the "fathers" of management books[64], pointed out that a strategy of diversity forces a decentralized structure **(structure follows strategy)**. It also has implications for other dimensions of an enterprise.

---

[63] Quoted by Alastair Campbell in *Winners and How they Succeed*, Hutchinson, Randon House, 2015.

[64] Chandler, Alfred D., *Strategy and Structure: Chapters in the History of the American Industrial Enterprise*, 1962.

I believe that one of the benefits of using the 7S framework flows from thinking about the **implications** of each dimension for each of the others. For example, if Alliances are a key element of your strategy, are you developing the skills, recruiting the staff and embedding a style that provides the necessary foundations for the strategy to be **successfully implemented**? An example of Interdependence.

There are many examples of companies that have developed and evolved strategies that have been enduring, with aligned structures and strongly shared values - for example GE (http://www.ge.com) and Innocent drinks (http://www.innocentdrinks.co.uk). The latter was launched in the UK in 1999 and acquired by Coca Cola in 2013). There are however many more enterprises with well thought out strategies, aligned structures and shared values that have not been successful. Consideration of the remaining 4 **7-Ss** can provide insights on the drivers of such success or failure.

Structure

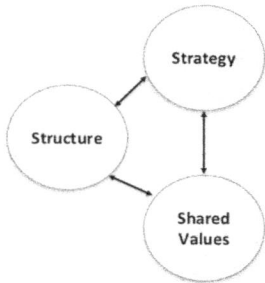

The building blocks of structure are tasks and coordination. Enterprises decide on tasks that should be performed by groups within the enterprise that are delivering to customers. Others are performed more centrally in some form of corporate department.

At a more detailed level, **tasks are broken down** into components that can be completed efficiently by some form of specialist and **then reintegrated** by a **coordinating mechanism** of some kind. For example, individuals may record the time they spend on a particular project (each individual working on the project is the **expert** on where his or time is being spent). Then a coordinating mechanism (an invoice clerk) brings together the details of all the time spent on a particular project, and any associated expenses, together with the client's details. They then raise the invoice. At a certain size and complexity the task may need to be **delegated** to a division to retain a maintainable span of control (the traditional answer). Following research in the 1990s, Robin Dunbar, an evolutionary psychologist / anthropologist, concluded that the

optimum size for a social group amongst humans was **about 150**[65]. Alternatively some form of shared service centre could be used, where additional coordination (potentially in the form of processes and technology), is established. This enables larger scale operations to be delivered, **effectively and efficiently**. Historically enterprises split tasks by geography and/or by function (for example, Finance, Legal, Human Resources, Marketing etc.). More recently some enterprises have placed the primary focus on managing by product or service line. Notwithstanding the approach to organisational structure, I encourage Directors to keep the **150 Dunbar Number** in mind as your organisations increase in size. In his book *More Human – Designing a World Where People Come First*, Steve Hilton highlights WL Gore & Associates, the most innovative materials company, (developer of GORETEX amongst other products) and the Tax Authority in Sweden. These two very different enterprises have used the 150 Dunbar number successfully to guide their decisions on structure.

With the rapid expansion of **matrix type** organisations, where for example geography and product organisations exist, the potential for duplication and ever more difficult coordination

---

[65] R. I. M. Dunbar (1993). *Coevolution of neocortical size, group size and language in humans*, Behavioral and Brain Sciences, 16, pp 681-694 doi:10.1017/S0140525X00032325

mushroomed. This was an important context for the **Business Process Re-engineering** (BPR) movement of the 1990s. The outcome of BPR initiatives in medium and large enterprises was often a move to tightly defined enterprise processes with **formal process owners**. These process owners are generally responsible for ensuring cross-function, cross-geography etc. performance effectively, and efficiently meets customer needs.

Notwithstanding the widespread adoption of both Business Process Re-engineering techniques and matrix organisations, sadly there are too many examples of **organisational silos** damaging organisational performance. Gillian Tett[66], a Financial Times Journalist, in her book on Organisational Silos describes Sony's attempts to replace their eminent **Sony Walkman music player**. The wealth of technology available to Sony in their **organisational Silos**, that had weak cross enterprise communication, resulted in the internal development of **two competing devices** that confused customers. At a similar time, Apple entered the market by launching their music player / music store combination. This quickly achieved a

---

[66] Tett, G., *The Silo Effect: Why putting everything in its place isn't such a bright idea*, Little Brown, London, 2015
http://www.amazon.co.uk/The-Silo-Effect-putting-everything-ebook/dp/B00GFHG2CM

dominance that left little space for either of the Sony products!

Leaders at all levels can have a powerful influence on how people develop their **personal networks across organisations**. For example, Tom Peters argues persuasively for people to use lunch as an opportunity to build relationships, outside ones immediate work group[67]. Not least perhaps because of the deep understanding they have from their data on peoples' behaviour, the Leadership of Facebook was particularly concerned about the impact of increasing size on their **corporate DNA**. Three of their initiatives resonate particularly strongly with me because I see parallels with my own experience – particularly as a Royal Air Force Officer. Facebook invests considerable resources in a six week **Boot camp** that **all** new employees attend. Whilst the primary objective was to get new joiners up to speed on the Facebook Code base, the Boot camp also **promoted good habits** and **created bonds** amongst the classmates. These persist after the individuals are spread across project teams. In the Royal Air Force (RAF) case, during officer training we were organised in **flights** that comprised a mix of specialities and genders. When I joined the RAF in the late 1970s, the mixed gender flights were being introduced and I recall the added dimension that such diversity

---

[67] Tom Peters, *Strategy:20x 12 =240*, https://youtu.be/DD_v7cbYN7k

introduced to leadership activities, and the strong competition between the mixed flights and the male only flights. A second parallel is the **movement of people**. Facebook moves their people between projects as a key anti silo measure. The RAF's process of moving people every 2 to 3 years had a similar effect (as well as experience building advantages etc.). Time in the Officers' Mess (eating, attending social events and perhaps particularly the Friday evening **Happy Hour**), provided numerous opportunities to **bump into people** from across different sections of the organisation. This facilitated **relationships** with people outside one's own team (Silo). Facebook use mechanisms such as Hackamonth deployments and six weekly hackathons to enhance further such horizontal communication. As Jocelyn Goldfein of Facebook stated to Gillian Tett:

"The power of knowing at least one person in each silo is crucial for making the company work"[68]

One trend that is particularly apparent in High Performing enterprises, is the **widespread use of project teams** (often with members from a spectrum of functional and geographic backgrounds). These teams focus on achieving specific, time bound, strategic tasks. Recent

---

[68] Tett, G., *The Silo Effect: Why putting everything in its place isn't such a bright idea*, Little Brown, London, 2015.

research conducted by John Kotter[69] has identified the use of **networks of willing volunteers alongside conventional hierarchies,** to **accelerate** the capacity to change. In these organisations, individuals contribute to change initiatives as part of the network as well as fulfilling roles in the line organisation.

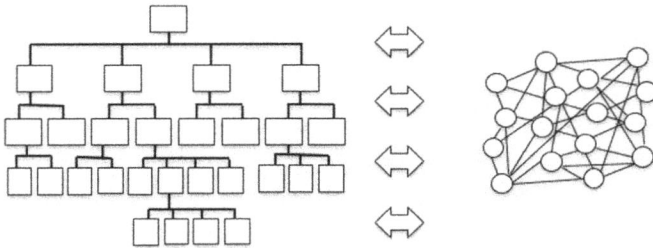

Figure 36: Networks of willing volunteers complement traditional organisational hierarchies

Kotter argues that such "dual operating systems" enable the data needed to turn threats into opportunities, to be processed with the agility that 20th Century hierarchical organisations find difficult, if not impossible.[70] I consider this as a practical example of implementing Christensen's (2016) point that "leaders can structure their organisations to allow the kinds of innovation that

---

[69] Kotter. J.P. , *Accelerate*, Harvard Business Review Press, 2014.

[70] Kotter. J.P., *Accelerate - The evolution of the 21st Century Organisation.* https://www.youtube.com/watch?v=Pc7EVXnF2aI

stave off disruption"; however as Satya Nadella, the CEO of Microsoft has acknowledged, the opposite is also true:

"Whenever you become good at maximizing past successes there can be a tendency to have less synergies .... the competition does not respect internal boundaries."[71]

Systems

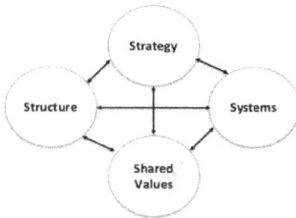

Systems include **formal and informal procedures, job aids and processes**, as well as the information / computer applications.

Collectively they are **how an enterprise gets things done**. These systems need to balance the need for effective governance across an enterprise, with sufficient flexibility for general managers serving local markets to **compete effectively**. Increasingly, computer based information systems enable enterprises to better **balance** the **demands of global efficiency** and **local responsiveness**.

---

[71] Tett, G., *The Silo Effect: Why putting everything in its place isn't such a bright idea*, Little Brown, London, 2015.

In many enterprises these information systems are a mix, with some systems hosted in **the cloud,** and others residing inside the enterprise. Recent research, has highlighted that enterprises that use a **common system** to facilitate a process to turn ideas into applications, are more agile. They can more rapidly create and test their ideas, and either **succeed or fail more quickly** (reducing costs in both cases).[72] In some enterprises a critical system will be the **technology platform** that **brings together buyers and sellers** of your products and services. eBay was an early example.

A mix of well-sponsored **continuous improvement** and **capability improvement** projects, can have a huge impact on the effectiveness of an organisation's systems. If, however, an enterprise's systems cannot generate efficiently the data needed to **support implementation** of the chosen strategy, inefficient **workarounds** and **temporary fixes** evolve. For example, an enterprise I was familiar with, generated the bulk of its revenues in the United States. Following the acquisition of another company, a cost reduction strategy was put in place. This included consolidating the accounting onto one system. The system chosen had proved

---

[72] Techradarpro blog, *Top five cloud trends for 2015: a new era of B2B innovation*, http://www.techradar.com/news/internet/cloud-services/top-five-cloud-trends-for-2015-a-new-era-of-b2b-innovation-1280677, 15 January 2015.

reliable and fit for purpose for the US business and a small volume of European projects. Following the acquisition there was a materially higher volume of projects across Europe. The system required manual actions to complete the accounting for these projects necessitating additional finance personnel. Furthermore, the Leadership Team's management information was delayed and **uncertainty over the accuracy** of manual interventions proved a **distraction**. This diverted leadership attention from the external marketplace. On the other hand knowledge sharing technology such as Slack,[73] can enable even the smallest enterprises to share knowledge cheaply, and thereby **minimise the risks** of damage from the silos discussed earlier.

Style

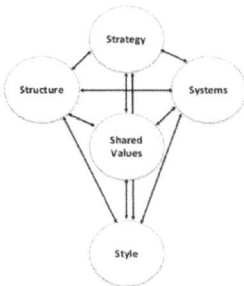

Variables under the 7-S style category include how managers **choose to spend their time** and their approach to interacting with others

---

[73] https://slack.com

Some top executives, signal in quite a **collaborative way**, what is on their mind (perhaps using Twitter, Yammer or other social media). They constantly **reinforce messages**, and **nudge** people in the **direction needed** to implement the selected tactics and strategy. Others may adopt a traditional command and control style.

The former may do this naturally, using up very little of the time in their hectic schedules. Others may spend much more time working on repeated drafts of formal updates. These are then subject to clearance by all the functional heads (Finance, HR, Legal, Marketing etc.), before circulation. This limits their capacity to give **Top Management Attention** to **anticipating** and **sensing emerging issues**.

I am seeing more and more written about the style and **values of leaders** being seen and perceived as **authentic**. Foundations for achieving this in my view include:

1. Physical and virtual **management by walking about**. This makes leaders more visible and encourages conversations with people at all levels across an enterprise. Promoting such interactions can both encourage engagement and **surface un-sandpapered assessments** from employees and other stakeholders, (rather than relying purely on commentary from

Enterprise Head Office). I have personally seen the value of this while working for a Commander-in-Chief in the Royal Air Force. The dialogues I witnessed were invaluable in helping the Commander-in-Chief anticipate and sense changes. They also gave individuals, at all levels, opportunities to hear first-hand perspectives on new capabilities and emerging requirements. The Commander-in-Chief concerned, had a most engaging style that made this easier to do authentically than perhaps would have been the case for some of his colleagues.

2. **Aligning** their style, consistently with the organisational structure, strategy, shared values (and indeed the other 7-S factors), recognising the evolving needs of the modern enterprise:

"I imagine the modern organisation as a three-dimensional hollow cube. The leader of today sits in the centre of the cube and, scattered around all six sides, are the product, geographic and functional entities that comprise the global corporation. Some of these are closer, emotionally and physically, to the CEO, while others are more remote. Within this complex hollow cube, the CEO can no longer hope to issue orders and to see them faithfully carried out. Indeed, all he or she can do is to exercise influence and steer this

writhing disparate mass of employees, customers, products and technologies towards the desired vision for the global business."

Iain Martin, 2013[74]

I believe that Style, from a 7-S perspective, also embraces an enterprise's **culture**. While an Associate Partner at Accenture I witnessed the change in one operating group when a new, very energetic, hands-on, Group CEO was appointed. She personally, and very visibly, sponsored a range of growth initiatives and provided **top cover** for individuals to **try new things with clients**. We built, remarkably quickly, a spectrum of new capabilities to replace the large historic systems development projects that had been the backbone of the group's work. This contrasted with my experience on the New Management Strategy initiative in the Ministry of Defence. While working on the implementation Team I researched the people aspects of the changes involved for my MBA dissertation. I concluded that full benefits of the strategy would not be gained without a culture change and that this was going to take time,

---

[74] http://www.ijmartin.com/noticeboard/

Staff

Three questions:

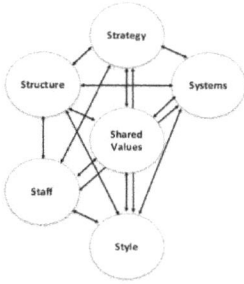

1. How do **you develop your first line supervisors**, and the people you believe have the capability of being your **future managers and leaders** (or do you "buy-in" skills as you need them)?

2. How do your **leading competitors develop their first line supervisors**, managers and the people they believe have the capability of being their future leaders?
3. How do you shape the basic values of your management team?

The original Peters, Waterman and Phillips research[75] highlighted that superbly organised companies pay **extraordinary attention to the people** joining their enterprise. They proactively manage a process to **socialise new recruits** into their enterprises, **manage their careers** and develop them into future managers. These processes include mechanisms to provide

---

[75] Peters. T, Phillips, J. Waterman. R, *Structure is not Organization*, Business Horizons, June 1980.

mentoring and counselling, well-orchestrated opportunities for **access to top management** and openings to participate in project teams. During my time at Accenture, we had well-structured induction programmes and actively engaged career counsellors. We also devoted serious top management effort to teaching our points of view on business issues / developments / challenges to more junior staff. Moreover, one of the four criteria for annual assessments was the development of people. Google believe that it is essential to recruit individuals who have the personal capability to grow with the rapidly expanding company. They therefore consider individual potential for two, three or four roles in the future when recruiting. How do you approach the recruitment and development of your people? To quote Peters, Waterman and Phillips[76]:

"Considering people as a pool of resources to be nurtured, developed, guarded and allocated is one of the many ways to turn the "staff" dimension of our 7-S framework into something not only amenable to, but worthy of practical control by senior management."

---

[76] Peters. T, Phillips, J. Waterman. R, *Structure is not Organization*, Business Horizons, June 1980.

Skills

Another Three questions:

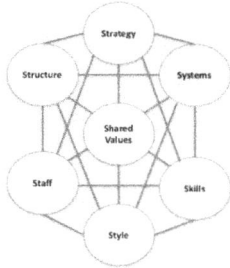

1. What does your enterprise **do best**?
2. What are the crucial **attributes** of your enterprise that enable you to deliver at your best today?
3. What are the crucial attributes of your enterprise that will enable you to deliver at your best **in 24 months time**?

In our agile world, enterprises frequently face changes in business conditions that **cannot be forecast from past trends**. These are sometimes referred to as discontinuities in management jargon. These necessitate more than a change in the strategic or tactical focus of an enterprise's people, and other resources. **New capabilities** are frequently going to be needed. This is likely to be much quicker in enterprises with "employees who are **capable of making independent decisions** about priorities that are consistent with the strategic direction and business model of the company."[77]

Some changes may result in **embedded skills becoming redundant**. One example, in the Information Systems industry, is the emergence of cloud services as a robust business alternative to running servers and their associated software in-house. In the short-term, the emergence of cloud services creates great opportunities for service providers to transition enterprises off their **in-house** systems. The skills developed in doing this may, however, become redundant as the wave of cloud transitions fade. A challenge for such enterprises will be to re-skill / up-skill their people so that they have relevant capabilities for the next wave of demand. Perhaps they can help their people develop business analytics skills to exploit the opportunities of ever-growing **big data**, as more and more devices connect to the Internet?

I am now going to return to an example mentioned in the strategy section above. If **alliances** are a **key element of your strategy**, are you acquiring the necessary skills to manage them effectively? Amongst the characteristics of successful partner managers identified in the "*Today's Alliance Professional....Tomorrow's Strategic Leader*" [78]study were:

---

[77] Christensen, C.M., *The Clayton M. Christensen Reader*, Harvard Business School Publishing Corporation, 2016.

- Ability to lead and influence
- Strategic/global thinkers seeking and creating opportunities
- Capable of dealing with high levels of ambiguity
- Highly innovative, dynamic, creative, independent thinkers
- People-oriented with high empathy
- Highly cooperative, preferring to work in teams
- Effective at networking across organizational boundaries

If alliances are a key part of your strategy, do you have **actions** for developing and retaining these skills?

Thinking more broadly, what efforts do you have underway to **re-tool** your staff, so that their skills are relevant to the future needs of your enterprise?

To conclude this discussion of the 7-S framework, I would like to leave you with three thoughts.

1. This framework is **tried and tested** and is not this year's fad!

---

[78] American Management Association, Society of Human Resource Management, and the Association of Strategic Alliance Professionals . *Today's Alliance Professional...Tomorrow's Strategic Leader*, 2009

2. I have found the framework the most applicable to the challenge of seeking to understand how **an enterprise really works**.

3. It provides a holistic basis for developing a broad scope of **actions** that will improve the probability of **successfully growing the agility** necessary to flourish in our rapidly changing world.

Developing your "To Be" Vision

"Scenario planning is a way of helping businesses to organise what they already know, or can easily discover, about the possible environment in which they will be working, say, five years ahead. It helps to add a framework to the process of strategic thinking."

Shell[79]

Scenario planning is a technique that can further inform your sense of developments in the market place. Some enterprises, such as Shell have invested major effort in generating very sophisticated scenarios; however, a very modest investment of time will help leadership teams improve their view of the **shape** of their **Market place in future**.

---

[79] http://www.shell-livewire.org/business-library/business-plans/why-you-need-a-business-plan/Scenario-planning/

"Rather than making forecasts, good scenario planners sketch out different possibilities and bring together people with different perspectives to work through the details. The end result will be several plausible, internally consistent and emotionally compelling stories about the future. The scenarios will highlight hidden connections and make distant consequences seem real. But, importantly, the scenarios will also contradict each other."

Tim Harford[80]

The key is to develop and apply **robust strategic thinking**. For example:

1. **Select** several (perhaps the top ten) **market forces** and **imagine related changes** that could **influence your enterprise**. For example an aging population, efforts by global industry enterprises to penetrate your business market segment or a significant competitor poaching your key staff. Scanning the business press and social media for key headlines, often suggests potential changes that might impact your enterprise. Discuss these and consider how potentially serious the impact is of each factor (**Impact Severity**). Then consider the likelihood of each of these factors occurring (**Probability**). To help your team focus I suggest you use your business judgment to

---

[80] *Brexit and the Power of Wishful Thinking* – Financial Times 13 July 2016.
https://next.ft.com/content/e8793d78-4880-11e6-8d68-72e9211e86ab

assign a number from 1 (low) to 10 (High) to each factor. You can then **rank** the **potential changes** and focus further thought on those that you identified as most important. Appling this technique at a small IT services company the following judgments were arrived at.

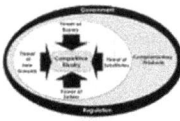

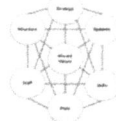

Driver	Source	Description & Impact on Enterprise	Impact Severity	Prob-ability	Rank
New Entrants to Market	Porter Analysis	Entry of small companies from low cost countries increase pricing pressure	-5	7	3
Substitute Products	Porter Analysis	Expansion of Cloud usage reduces demand for IT projects	-4	9	1
Institutions	PESTLEI & 7S Analysis	Establishment of Chartered IT Profession necessities additional staff training	-3	5	6
Political	PESTLEI Analysis	Additional regulation increases demand for compliance systems	+3	9	4
Technical	PESTLEI Analysis	Widespread adoption of SDN increases demand for network services	+3	5	5
Social	PESTLEI Analysis	Increased concern for data security increased demand for network services	+5	9	1

Figure 37: Scenarios: drivers, impact, probability and rankings

2. For each change in a force, discuss **three different future scenarios**, (best case, worst case, and highest probability / mid case) which **could impact** the enterprise. Debating the worst-case scenario often

provokes a readiness to consider changing / evolving the strategic direction of the enterprise.

3. Suggest **potential strategies / tactics** the enterprise could adopt in each of the three scenarios to respond to each change.

4. **Select** the highest probability changes that could have the greatest impact on the enterprise over the next three to five years, and identify the **most appropriate strategies** the enterprise could undertake to exploit / mitigate the changes.

The following graphics show how this technique can be implemented:

External Forces Driving Changes	Impact of External Force on your Enterprise		
	Best Case	Worst Case	Highest Probability Case
Force 1			
	Strategic / Tactical Response	Strategic / Tactical Response	Strategic / Tactical Response
Force 2			
	Strategic / Tactical Response	Strategic / Tactical Response	Strategic / Tactical Response
Force 3			
	Strategic / Tactical Response	Strategic / Tactical Response	Strategic / Tactical Response
Force 4			
	Strategic / Tactical Response	Strategic / Tactical Response	Strategic / Tactical Response

Figure 38: Scenarios: Driving forces

Using the **highest ranked** drivers in step 1 and the accompanying table the following conclusions might be reached:

External Forces Driving Change driving	Impact of External Force on your Enterprise		
	Best Case	Worst Case	Highest Probability Case
New small company competitors from low cost countries	Your clients require significant face to face time and are concerned about security of data and Intellectual Property	Clients retender all projects and select lowest cost provider.	Loss of some price sensitive clients to small low cost providers
	Strategic / Tactical Response	Strategic / Tactical Response	Strategic / Tactical Response
	Increase face to face interactions. Brief all clients on location of their data and arrangements for protecting this and any of their IP that you have access to.	Simplify projects and report. Determine price at which you "walk away" to protect the economics of your business	Increase frequency of face to face interactions with clients. Brief all clients on location of their data and arrangements for protecting this and any of their IP that you have access to. Demonstrate the speed of your responsiveness and the benefits of a local provider

External Forces Driving Change driving	Impact of External Force on your Enterprise		
	Best Case	Worst Case	Highest Probability Case
Additional regulation increases demand for compliance systems	During a client meeting you identify a new compliance system projects & secure it as an extension to existing work.	Your capabilities are not considered adequate for compliance projects	Clients invite you to submit proposals for new compliance system projects.
	Strategic / Tactical Response	Strategic / Tactical Response	Strategic / Tactical Response
	Use project to develop capabilities inc. skills and reusable IP	Develop a written point of view on the success factors for compliance projects. Highlight how you have the capabilities to address these.	Identify relevant experience and skills that are transferable to compliance projects and any relevant projects you can quote. Identify decision makers and influencers at the client. Appoint members of your team to "tag" each of these.

External Forces Driving Change driving	Impact of External Force on your Enterprise		
	Best Case	**Worst Case**	**Highest Probability Case**
Additional regulation increases demand for compliance systems	*During a client meeting you identify a new compliance system project & secure it as an extension to existing work.*	*Your capabilities are not considered adequate for compliance projects*	*Clients invite you to submit proposals for new compliance system projects.*
	Strategic / Tactical Response	Strategic / Tactical Response	Strategic / Tactical Response
	Use project to develop capabilities inc. skills and reusable IP	*Develop a written point of view on the success factors for compliance projects. Highlight how you have the capabilities to address these.*	*Identify relevant experience and skills that are transferable to compliance projects and any relevant projects you can quote. Identify decision makers and influencers at the client. Appoint members of your team to "tag" each of these.*

Figure 39: Scenarios: Examples of external forces

Vision

Your consideration of the **varied scenarios** for your market place, provides a foundation for revisiting the vision you have for your enterprise. A **sharp vision**, relevant to the envisaged market environment and **really understandable** to the people in your enterprise, can make a material contribution to increasing motivation. In his Forbes blog[81], Joseph Folkman articulates the positive impact, when employees can see **how their work contributes** to realising the company's vision:

"Employees who don't find their company's vision meaningful at all have average engagement scores of only 16 per cent. These are employees who do not care about

---

[81] Folkman, J., *8 Ways to ensure that your vision is valued*, http://www.forbes.com/sites/joefolkman, 22 April 2014.

the future success of the organization. They work primarily for a pay check and are willing to do very little beyond what is absolutely required to keep their jobs. Those who find their organizations' vision meaningful have engagement levels that are 18 percentile points above average."
Joseph Folkman

Following his observations of numerous enterprises trying to communicate their visions, John Kotter[82] has argued for a different approach, that he calls the **Big Opportunity**. It is explained to employees in words that are emotionally engaging and paint a picture of a prosperous, winning future.

"It is related to vision and strategy in a very straightforward way: a strategy shows you what you need to get to a vision; a vision shows you what you will be doing if you get to, and are able to capitalize on, a big opportunity."
John Kotter

Strategic Gap

The gap between the current enterprise **As Is**, and the **picture of future success** that you painted as you analysed the competitive environment and your own enterprise, represents a "**strategic gap**". Developing thoughtful actions to close this strategic gap are the next steps on our climb.

---

[82] Kotter, J.P., *Forget the Strategy PowerPoint*, HBR Blog Network, 22 April 2014.

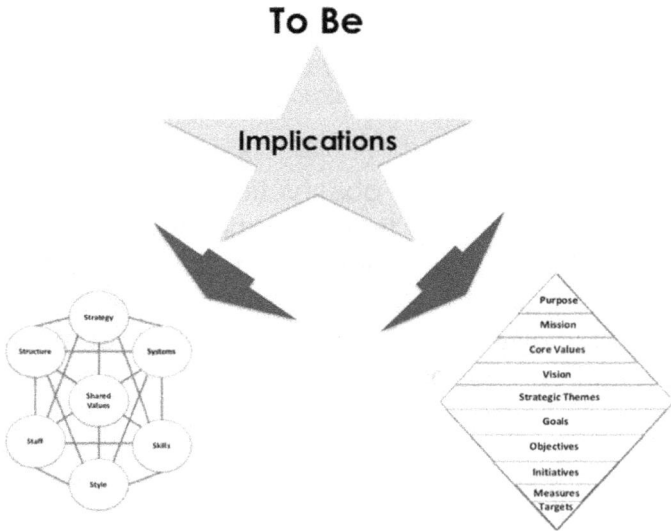

Figure 40: Implications of your "To Be"

In the next sections, I include **Strategic Themes**, **Goal Setting** and the **Future Wheel** technique, as tools that will help translate your picture of the future into sustainable actions. I will return to the Strategic Gap concept in the later discussion of forecasting.

Strategic Themes

Defining three or four high-level strategic themes, that break the strategic gap into actionable focus areas, provides a **logical basis** for **setting goals and objectives**. These then lead to complementary initiatives that move the enterprise in the agreed strategic direction, (rather than causing **organisation death through 100 uncoordinated initiatives**). In one of the enterprises I served, the strategic themes were operational excellence, strategic partnering, excellent client service and a compelling place to work. We believed that these strategic themes were our **pillars of excellence**. When you identify one strategic result, from one strategic theme, you create a manageable basis for developing the enterprise. This is easier to implement than the very detailed strategic plans that I have seen in some organisations.

I find it helpful to develop this thinking into a **strategy story** that is used to **communicate** the **things to be done,** throughout the enterprise. One approach to injecting real richness into this story is to appoint **subject matter experts** for each theme. These experts use their experience to break each theme into a set of strategic objectives. Each objective is mapped to your **point of view** on how the enterprise will **create value** for your customers and other stakeholders. This can be illustrated in a **strategy map** (see below), that validates the coherence of your objectives. You can then use the map to **communicate the strategy** to all your people.

The following example is for an information systems consulting enterprise that identified operational excellence, building [growing] the business and understanding stakeholders (including customers) as three strategic themes. These were the result of robust discussions during a **strategy day**. Note that the diagram includes objectives (with arrows to illustrate cause and effect), prioritisation of some of the objectives and segmentation in four dimensions to help implementation – Financial, Stakeholders, Business Processes and Employees & Infrastructure. The Enterprise now uses these 4 dimensions in a **Balanced Scorecard** to assess performance each month. At the top of the diagram there is space to enter the enterprise purpose, mission, core values and vision. These can then easily be referred to as **strategic themes** and **aligned goals** can then be discussed.

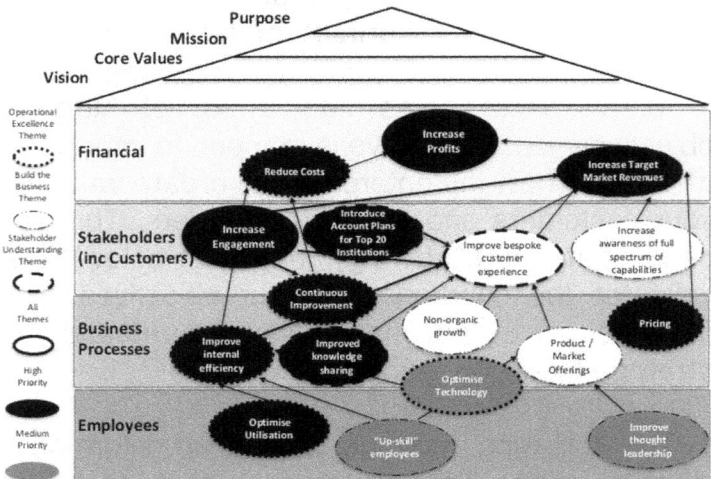

Figure 41: An example of a strategy map

In my experience, a key to **achieving value** from investing effort to develop such themes, is the transparency between **objectives** and **initiatives,** the stated **values** of the organisation, and the stated enterprise **strategy**. This necessitates employees **understanding the values** of the enterprise AND sensing the linkage to the initiatives they are **investing their time in**. Engaging environments **inspire discretionary effort**. To achieve and maintain them, Leaders need to **demonstrate values** that **resonate with a spectrum of enterprise stakeholders** (as opposed perhaps to only some of the employees' wallets). Personally I have been fortunate to see the benefits that flow from the culture that emerges – not least during my time on 16 Squadron in the Royal Air Force and at Andersen Consulting / Accenture. Both organisations were less reliant on checks to ensure process compliance, were more creative and most importantly, were able to **maintain strategic direction** through **fogs** of intense competitive rivalry.

Institutionalizing the capacity to change

"Organisations need people who can meet the dual demands of discipline and stretch."

Ghoshal and Barlett 1994[83]

Before discussing implementation of actions, five comments about change processes.

1. Organisations that approach change initiatives with a **Learning Mind-set** are much more likely to institutionalise the capacity to change effectively, into their DNA.

2. Change is unsettling and individuals need **support and time** to learn and implement new ways of working. Some decline in enterprise performance should be planned to avoid unfortunate surprises / unplanned budget variances.

3. Visible, on-going **sponsorship** of the change process, and the new ways of working by Leaders at all levels, helps people recognise that the changes are real and not just **flavour of the week**. Furthermore, it is vital to set **clear expectations,** that efficient **optimisation** of current performance, **innovation** and effective development / change management of **new capabilities,** are necessary. Professor Jane McKenzie of Henley Business School refers to this as

---

[83] Ghoshal. Sumantra, Barlett, Christopher A., *Linking organizational context and managerial action: The dimensions of quality of management*, 1994.

"Developing Ambidexterity: A Leadership Challenge to Engage Both Sides of the Organisational Brain".

4. Done well, the change processes themselves help develop your **next generation of leaders**, at all levels in the organisation.

5. **Involving** your high performers in the development of the new processes, systems and perhaps as **super users,** represents a **win-win** for both the **individual and the enterprise**. During my time at Accenture we had an Action Learning programme for the next generation of Partners in one of the operating groups. This involved the identification and development of capabilities needed for our evolving marketplace.

Your "To Be"

"Plan for your future because that is where you are going to spend the rest of your life"
Mark Twain

Armed with:

- your **positioning** of your enterprise on its **S-Curves**,

- an assessment of the competitive environment (from the Porter **5 Force** and **PESTELI** analyses),
- your considerations of your organisational effectiveness (from your **7-S analysis**)
- your thinking about different **scenarios** for your enterprise in your competitive environment,

you are now in a position to make a more **informed judgement of future potential**. One start point is to consider, in revenue terms, **three alternative futures**:

- Business as usual (the initial forecast).
- Revenues that can be achieved if full commitment is made to **continuous improvement** actions (the revised forecast).
- Revenues that you assess are achievable if you become **more agile** and evolve your **strategic direction**. This should include realistic assumptions on how successful you will be in building the capabilities needed to execute the change (the corporate objective).

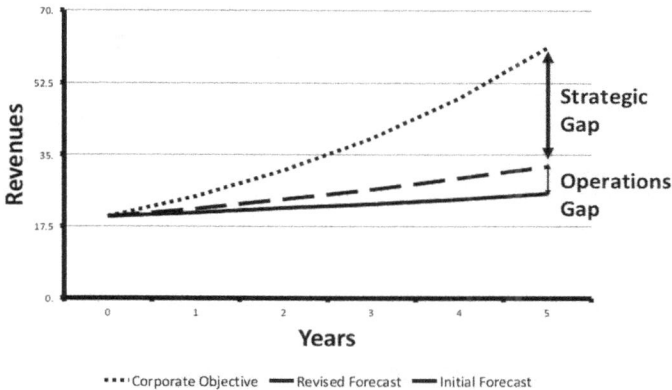

Figure 42: Strategic and operations gaps

The **strategic themes** identified should help you set **goals** that will close the strategic gap shown on the chart above. For example, you may have concluded that you are not optimally pricing your products / services and this could form one of your goals. An **objective** to help achieve this goal could be a 3% improvement in the margin on new contracts. This could be supported by an **initiative** to develop a new pricing tool that would enable all relevant costs to be built into estimates more efficiently and consistently. Putting **measures and targets** in place will then enable the management team to assess progress in achieving the goal. On a frequent (monthly) basis, adjustments to resources or tactics can be agreed. Needless to say, this will only hold good if the **measures are**

appropriate. It is consequently prudent to remember to:

Measure the **RIGHT THING**

in the **RIGHT WAY**

=

the **RIGHT RESULT**

Moreover I suggest that you only delegate the development of measures to individuals who understand the Purpose, Mission, Core Values and Vision for the enterprise. Keep in mind:

"There are risks and costs in a program of action, but they are far less than the long-range risks and costs of comfortable inaction"

John F. Kennedy[84]

Returning to the **strategic diamond** that I introduced earlier, I encourage you to reflect on a business change that YOU have introduced. Consider the extent to which there was a **transparent** and **coherent rationale** that linked:

- the targets and measures used to assess business performance

---

[84]

http://news.google.com/newspapers?id=QOgzAAAAIBAJ&sjid=g4HAAAAIB AJ&dq=americans+for+democratic+action&pg=7056%2C2944411

- initiatives,
- objectives,
- goals,
- strategic themes,

to the **visions**, core **values**, **mission** and **purpose** at the top of the diamond.

Figure 43: Efficienarta Strategic Diamond

Reducing "Unintended Consequences"

Initiative Planning

Too often during my business life I have heard the criticism that colleagues considered we were going to suffer death from 100 **uncoordinated initiatives**. Taking for a moment the position that

perception is reality I see three sources for such criticisms:

a. Leaders had **not explained** how the initiatives would contribute to achieving the enterprise vision, OR

b. The initiatives **were uncoordinated**, OR

c. Unintended consequences **emerged** during the life of the initiatives.

I believe that the **strategic theme** approach outlined above, coupled with the "**Strategic Diamond**" breakdown to the level of measures and targets, should address points a and b. I am therefore going to focus this section on a technique to reduce the likelihood of unintended consequences from initiatives. The use of this technique, combined with the establishment of rigorous checkpoints to validate whether initiatives underway are still relevant[85], will reduce the probability of your colleagues suggesting **death by 100 uncoordinated initiatives**.

---

[85] This is more and more of an issue in our rapidly changing world. In one consulting organisation I have worked with, a business review identified that 120 originally well sponsored initiatives were no longer relevant to the market.

Futures Wheel

Jerome Glenn of the Antioch Graduate School of Education in New England created the **Futures Wheel** technique[86] to identify visually the **potential consequences** of trends and events. Over the years it has also been used successfully in decision making to choose between options and in change management to identify the consequences of change. The technique is a useful complement to unstructured brainstorming, as it **helps organise thinking** and provoke **relevant questions**, rather than encourage participants to list the first consequences that occur to them.

A **Futures Wheel** starts with a short **statement of the change** to be evaluated in the centre of a blank piece of paper. Then, events or **consequences** following directly from that development are positioned around it. Next, the **indirect consequences** of the direct consequences are positioned around the first level consequences. This process then continues for third and forth level consequences etc.

The following steps show how a Futures Wheel can be constructed:

---

[86] Glenn, J. C., *Futures Wheel, Futures Research Methodology Version 3.0*, The Millennium Project, Washington, D.C. 2009.

Write the change that you need to consider in the centre of a flip chart or a blank sheet of paper. This could be an event, a trend, a problem, or a possible solution to a business issue.

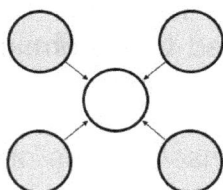

Brainstorm possible direct consequences of that change. Write each consequence in a circle, and connect it from the central idea with an arrow. For example, the direct consequences of imposing a 15% budget cut could be the cancellation of an IT enhancement project, no external training, a hiring freeze and restrictions on travel expenditure (including perhaps staff flying on low cost airlines).

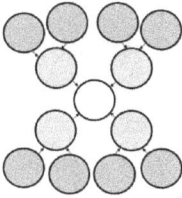

Brainstorm all the possible "second-order" consequences of each of the first-order (direct) consequences. For example the consequences of a hiring freeze maybe an inability to replace retiring staff, a delay in the recruitment of a planned office manager and no work for the recruitment manager.

This process is then repeated until the potential consequences are exhausted.

A completed Futures Wheel for the 15% budget cut issue mentioned above is as follows:

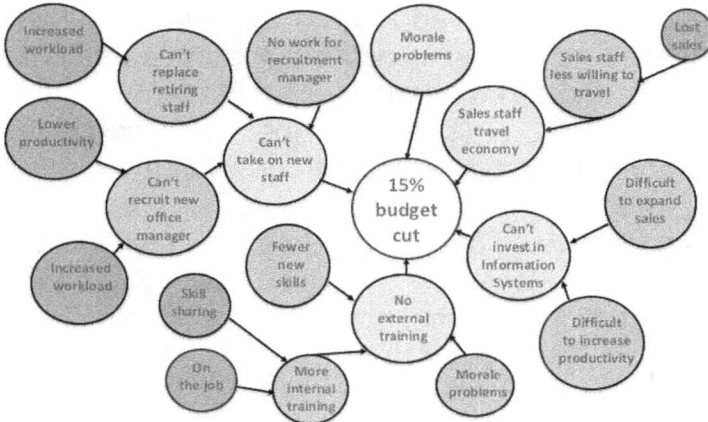

Figure 44: An example of a futures wheel

Please note how the **interconnecting lines** can make it easier to **visualize interrelationships** of the causes and resulting changes. By focusing attention on **direct and indirect consequences**, "Futures Wheels" can assist in developing ideas and options in a thoughtful way. Moreover, in the process they **reduce the likelihood of unintended consequences** surfacing as you develop the capabilities needed to execute your strategy.

Black Swans

Back in the 16th Century there was an assumption in London that all swans were white because the data available indicated that all known swans had white feathers. Sometime later an explorer identified a swan with Black Feathers in Australia and assumptions about the colour of swans had to be changed! The Black Swan term became a metaphor for a **perceived impossibility** that is **later disproven.** It was used by Nassim Taleb in his books "Fooled by Randomness: The Hidden Role of Chance in Life and in the Markets" [87] and "The Black Swan: The Impact of the Highly Improbable"[88]. Nassim Taleb

---

[87] Taleb, N.N, *Fooled by Randomness: The Hidden Role of Chance in Life and in the Markets,* 2004.

[88] Taleb, N.N, *The Black Swan: The Impact of the Highly Improbable,* 2007.

assesses almost all major discoveries as **black swans**, including the development of the Personal Computer and the Internet.

Surprise events will occur, however astute your analysis of your operating environment and your enterprise performance. In our relatively recent past, even large companies like Microsoft were caught off guard by the advance of the Internet. In hindsight it could be argued that the data was available to indicate the Internet's significance. The importance in the context of this discussion is two-fold:

1. We need to grow in our leaders the capacity to recognize **unknown unknowns** (to use Donald Rumsfeld's explanation from the days of the second Gulf War) i.e. events that lie outside the realm of regular expectations, because nothing in the past can convincingly point to the possibility of the event. Emmanuel Fabour, the CEO of Danone makes this point in a Leadership article in the Financial Times[89]

"I have learned to become very alert to blind spots .... So I try to maintain a balance in my schedule to connect myself with a very wide array of people."

---

[89] *Emmanuel Faber, Danone CEO on the alert for blind spots*, Financial Times, 4 April 2016.

For example, he chose to attend a World Social Forum in Brazil rather than the annual World Economic Forum in Switzerland.

2. We need to build enterprises that are **resilient and agile enough to exploit such events** and search for new competitive advantages quickly – before our competitors or new entrants to the market do.

Adaptive Planning - Agility without Anarchy

The effort devoted to administering the planning processes, in many of the enterprises I have worked with, saps the energy of executives and distracts them from more strategic thinking. This leads too often to assumptions based on the current year performance, rather than forecasts that recognise the changing nature of their marketplace. A key question for Directors is "**How to generate forecasts**" effectively. In my experience, a good start point can be a well facilitated workshop provided that it includes:

a. a concise explanation of the current strategic direction of the enterprise,

b. current enterprise performance data,

c. your own **internal experts** views on anticipated developments in each current product / service segment and developed using the tools and techniques introduced earlier in this chapter,

d. an authoritative external view of the evolution of your industry.

Philip Tetlock, a recognized global forecasting expert and a professor at the Wharton School in the United States of America, believes that

*"**foxes** - people who know a lot but do not believe in a single world view - predict the future better than specialists. In my experience, employees with diverse networks are likely to be foxes."*
Financial Times 19 May 2016

In many organisations the planning, budgeting and monthly review processes can be nightmares involving masses of Excel spread sheets. Too frequently, management time is wasted in **arguments over the accuracy of data** in spreadsheets, caused by **formula maintenance** issues, and **version control** problems. Particularly when different people make simultaneous modifications. This is not helped by the overall **brittle nature** of even the best-designed spread sheets. In these circumstances the planning and budgeting process itself can become an **enemy of agility**.

"Companies still using spread sheets for budgeting and forecasting are crippled by broken links, data integrity issues, and version control errors."

Adaptive Insights[90]

I have seen **heavily siloed** enterprises where the finance department is adamant that plans and budgets must be **locked down** by a given date and then not reopened until the next year's planning round (or if one is lucky, at the end of the first quarter). During my period as a Chief of Staff of a consultancy company, I became convinced that enterprises could no longer afford this **barrier to effectiveness**. I now consider investment in tools, processes and training that enable a **5-quarter rolling forecast approach** to be institutionalized, essential operating cost in our agile world. Amongst the companies taking this approach is Danone. They have replaced annual plans with such rolling forecasts that allow more flexibility. "It is the notion of not even being interested in the budget but having a constant ability to **reallocate non fixed resources**"[91]. Moreover, this needs to include efficient, effective, and consistent generation of financial reports after each accounting period. This is the foundation for **management actions** to be taken **quickly** so that they influence performance in the next period.

---

[90] http://www.adaptiveinsights.com/offer/demo-responsive/
[91] *Emmanuel Faber, Danone CEO: on the alert for blind spots,* Danone CEO Financial Times, 4 April 2016, "

Whist I have been a great fan of spread sheets since the early days of Lotus 123 and Supercalc, I believe that they are **no longer fit for purpose** for collaborative planning and budgeting in the second decade of the 21st century. A good selection of cost-effective specialist planning tools are now available for enterprises of all sizes. These enable more robust management / update of assumptions, easier collaboration, better productivity and a **focus on what one set of consistent numbers mean** (rather than wasting executive energy arguing about the correctness or otherwise of various versions of the numbers). Armed with one of these software tools, early each financial period, leaders can discuss the business with the benefit of solid numbers. The focus can immediately be on **reasons for variances and actions to close them**. At a minimum quarterly, the enterprise leaders can **reassess the competitive environment** and adjust the planning assumptions that drive the budgets. **Agility without anarchy**!

For example, at Thiess Mining in Australia[92], the Cloud Software "Adaptive Insights", enables shift management to **quickly analyse** shift performance on tablet computers in the field. They then make **resource adjustments** or initiate other necessary actions immediately. These are coordinated across the enterprise with the help of

---

[92] http://www.adaptiveinsights.com/uploads/docs/AP_Casestudy_Thiess.pdf

real time sharing of performance date. Staff across 25+ locations, access 40 different metrics derived from over eight million records, to obtain **insights on performance in seconds**. Within the first week of using this application, information gathered from the company's fleet of trucks identified a mechanical problem that could have significantly slowed production. An amazing contrast with the labour and spread sheet intensive processes of the past and a **real facilitator of agility**.

With the increasing **uncertainties** present in operating environments, I am surprised that many management teams insist on continuing to focus on **establishing forecasts in terms of a single value.** For example, sales in the next quarter will be Euros 4.5M (or year on year growth will be 10.5% etc.). I suggest that the one thing we can be sure about is that such forecasts will be wrong! Would an understanding of the likely **range of forecast** outcomes (probability adjusted) be a more helpful aid to **decision making**?

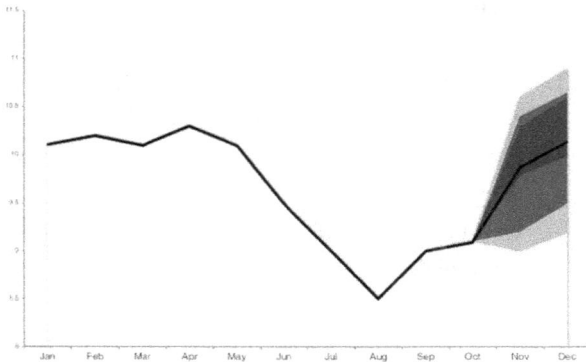

Figure 45: Forecast with a probability fan

In their *Harvard Business School Blog "A Simple Tool for Making Better Forecasts"*[93] Don Moore and Uriel Haran explain a method they have developed entitled SPIES (Subjective Probability Interval EStimates). Their method is designed to *"protect forecasters from the known traps of overconfidence and biased forecasting, and provide an informative forecast that includes plausible future scenarios as well as an assessment of how likely each one of them is to occur."* To use the SPIES method to determine a

---

[93] Moore. D., & Haran, U., *A Simple Tool for Making Better Forecasts*, HBR Blog, 19 May 2014.

forecast of net revenues for the case used in the graphic above:

a. Assess the maximum (perhaps 11.5 million Euros) and minimum (perhaps 8.5 million Euros) revenues for the forecast period.

b. Decide on the intervals for the estimates – perhaps 0.5M Euros.

c. For each month in the forecast period, estimate the probability of the net revenues (in Euros M) being between:

- 8.5 and 9
- 9 and 9.5
- 9.5 and 10
- 10 and 10.5
- 10.5 and 11
- 11 and 11.5

d. Based on this information produce a Fan diagram, such as the one above, to help communicate the probability weighted forecast estimates.

This technique also provides a foundation for measuring the accuracy of forecasts (dynamically in each forecast period). Moreover, if this measurement is based on the accuracy of individual sales people, unexpected variances can serve as "an early warning radar".

"If disruption is hitting your market, some sales people will be on top of this and their accuracy will stay good. Other sales people who are blind-sided by change will see a drop off in their accuracy ratings. By measuring accuracy dynamically, the company accuracy does not suffer."

Bernard Lunn[94]

Using this approach, executives keep in the forefront of their minds, the **range of potential outcomes**. They are then more alert to the likelihood of needing to make decisions to re-optimize operational efficiency as key variables change. I believe that approaches such as this can help executives improve the agility of their enterprises by better balancing effectiveness and efficiency.

Conclusions

"High performing organizations are distinguished by having the ability to "perceive changes in their external environment; test possible responses; and implement changes in products, technology, operations, structures, systems and capability as a whole."

Williams, Worley, Lawler III [95]

Our world is changing fast and **enterprises that are agile will be more likely to flourish**.

---

[94] Lunn, B., *Mindshare to Marketshare*, Amazon, 2014.

[95] Williams, T., Worley, C.G., & Lawler., E.G., *The Agility Factor*, Strategy + Business, 15 April 2013.

Underpinning the discussion in this chapter, is my personal belief that leaders / managers / supervisors with a **forward-thinking mind-set**, are already on the first step in their climb towards greater strategic agility. I hope that the tools I have introduced will help you to broaden your thinking about the **future of your enterprise**. Moreover, that they provide you with practical techniques for the next steps of your **ascent to more agile capabilities**.

To maintain an appropriate focus during your climb, I suggest that you endeavour to use consistently the following **3 Ds**.

1. Discussion:

"while it's rarely possible to eradicate all the internal barriers within an organization, it is possible to counter their effects by establishing cross-company systems to gather intelligence."[96]

Seek opinions and advice from your employees, customers, suppliers and other stakeholders:

- What do they think you are good at doing?
- What can be done better?

---

[96] Watkins, M.D., Bazerman, M.H., *Predictable Surprises – The Disasters that you should have seen coming*, Harvard Business Review, March 2003.

- Where do they see the industry in 3 years' time?
- What are the competitors doing?

2. Decision:

What is the **Biggest Opportunity** for the enterprise?

3. Development

- **Involve your people** in your planning efforts – including ideally a network of willing volunteers (as envisaged by John Kotter[97])
- **Visibly sponsor** and champion the **capabilities** you have identified as necessary to improve your enterprise performance and climb towards the **To Be** you have identified.
- Maintain a **transparent linkage** from the targets you set up through the levels of the strategic diamond **to your enterprise purpose.**

Most of all, **actions need to be implemented more quickly** than back in the days of stable

---

[97] Kotter, J.P, *Accelerate – How the most innovative capitalize on today's rapid-fire strategic challenges and still make their numbers*, Harvard Business Review, November 2012.

industry and competitive conditions. A June 2014 article in *The Economist* provided an overview of one of the initiatives that **GE** is taking to achieve this, entitled **FastWorks**. It focuses on launching new products earlier, seeking customer feedback faster and quickly improving the product.

"An early example of FastWorks in action involved a proposal by GE's engineers for a five-year, $500m project to upgrade its H-class gas turbine. Mr Immelt [Jack Welch's successor as GE CEO] called for the new approach to be applied, starting with a proof-of-concept exercise costing $25m. The result, GE says, is an upgrade that should be ready in two years for half the original cost."

The Economist, "A Hard Act To Follow", 28 June 2014

When **proactive development** of enterprise agility is combined with **effective engagement** of stakeholders and **effective continuous improvement**, we have a stronger foundation for sustained enterprise growth. To quote Clayton Christensen (2016):

*"Executives whose companies are currently making lots of money ought not to wonder **whether** the power to earn attractive profits will shift, but **when**. If they watch for the signals quite possibly they can prosper...."*

Please activate the QR code below (or type http://wp.me/P3ep12-tl into your browser) to reach a web page containing a number of templates and useful links to further information.

4 BUILDING STAKEHOLDER ENGAGAMENT

"More companies understand that a broader spectrum of internal and external stakeholders has a direct impact on their core business. Those that have engendered deep levels of engagement – what I call high relationship engagement – are far more successful in shaping that impact to their advantage."

Nadine B Hack – Executive in Residence IMD (2011)

The premises for this chapter are:

1. Our competitive world is **less certain**, has mounting **performance pressure**, increasing demands for **sustainability**, and in many cases a need to deliver excellent

customer experiences with **less loyal workers**.

2. **Engaging all stakeholders** and potential partners will improve enterprises' capability to **sense changes** in the competitive environment and spot opportunities and new sources of competitive advantage.

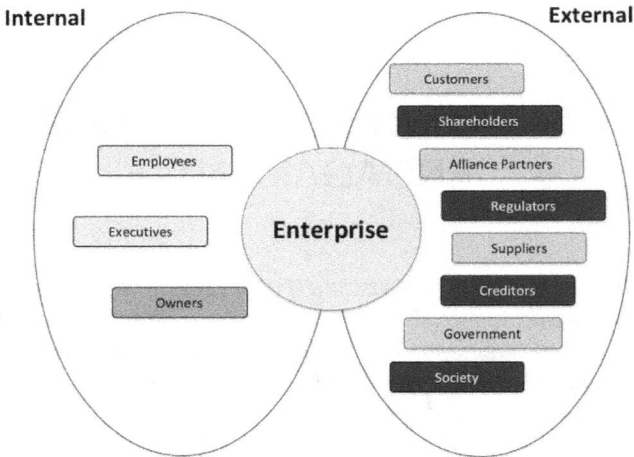

Figure 46: Internal and External Stakeholders

3. Both **continuous improvement** to existing products and services, and improving **enterprise agility** to capitalise on changes in the competitive market[98], are more

---

[98] Widen, K., Olander, S., Atkin, B. identified in *"Links Between Successful Innovation Diffusion and Stakeholder engagement"*, Journal of Management

successful when individuals **proactively engage**. Securing this **positive discretionary behaviour** can be the key to success.

4. The **relationship** between society and enterprises is fostered by enterprise behaviour that **encourages trust**, and avoids excesses that can undermine the foundations of capitalism.

The unprecedented level of **cooperation and interdependence** across enterprises creates an ever-stronger argument for building commitment across enterprise stakeholders.

*"Today, the term **stakeholder engagement** is emerging as a means of describing a broader, more inclusive, and continuous process between a company and those they impact, that encompasses a range of positive activities and approaches."*

International Finance Corporation (2007)

Sustainable success is the objective of building this **stakeholder commitment**, rather than merely short-term profit maximisation. Combining this trend, with the increasing prospects for extracting value from the data involved, can create

in Engineering, 11 May 2013 that "a structured process of engagement has to be an integral part of the innovation process. Accordingly an explicit plan for communication and engagement with identified key stakeholders is necessary Ex Ante as a condition for successful innovation and diffusion."

opportunities for building new business platforms. These **new business platforms** may extend across a number of separate enterprises. They can improve the **effectiveness** of existing business processes, as well as create opportunities for completely **new services**. For example **JustPark** (https://www.justpark.com) has developed a platform comprising people with car parking spaces (both traditional parking providers and individuals with space on their home drive ways etc.), which individuals requiring a car park space can access. As well as **improving the efficiency** of finding car park spaces, the platform enables individuals with spare space for cars to obtain an income from this **under-utilized resource**. Needless to say spaces close to railway stations, airports, sports stadiums etc. are particularly valuable once a means of matching buyers and sellers is established. In this case, the stakeholders involved extend to a car manufacturer that includes the application in their car navigation system.

For enterprises to have the **freedom to operate and innovate,** society needs to believe that such a **license is justified**. For example, it is essential for enterprises that gain value from using sensitive personal data, to safeguard this data. This necessitates:

- investing in appropriate **technology** and **processes,**

- ensuring that the people permitted access to this data are of sufficient **integrity,**
- Individuals are adequately **trained**,
- Working **practices** are audited to ensure compliance with agreed procedures etc.

*"Engagement is not an end in itself, but a means to help build **better relationships** with the societies in which we operate, ultimately resulting in **improved business planning and performance.**"*

Altria Corporate Services, Inc.[99]

In this chapter I will start by discussing **Trust** and **Justness** as a foundation for developing business relationships. I will then argue for executives to **focus on more than shareholder value**, before discussing expectations. I will then examine options for improving **stakeholder engagement**, with each of the groups identified above.

Trust and Justness

"A person "like yourself" is now trusted nearly two times as much as a CEO or government official."

Ben Boyd, Edelman 2015

We are in a particular interesting period. Trust between individuals who do not know each other appears to be reaching new heights. For example,

---

[99] *Stakeholder Engagement Planning – Overview.* Available from: http://www.forumstrategies.com/content/pdf/stakeholder_engagement.pdf

homes being rented via airbnb[100] to individuals without any previous relationship with the owner. On the other hand, individuals' trust with established institutions is falling. In his 10 August 2016 Financial Times column, Tim Harford articulates the critical role that trust plays:

"Steve Knack, an economist at the World Bank with a long-standing interest in trust, once told me that if one takes a broad enough view of trust, "it would explain basically all the difference between the per capita income of the United States and Somalia". In other words, without trust — and its vital complement, trustworthiness — there is no prospect of economic development."

The public relations firm Edelman, undertakes research across 27 nations to produce a *Trust Barometer.* The 2015 edition highlights that approximately two-thirds of respondents assessed trust in government, business, media and non-governmental organisations to be at the distrustful end of the scale. Following a survey of 700 wealthy well educated and well informed individuals, Shannon Bond reported in the *Financial Times* (20 January 2015) *that,* **only 57% of respondents trusted business** (down from 59% a year earlier). In *"Return on Trust" The Business Case* (2015), Barbara Brooks Kimmel argues that in the short term businesses can survive without trust but in the longer term enterprises that **embrace trust,** as both a

---

[100] https://www.airbnb.com

business imperative and a long-term strategy are **more likely to flourish**. The foundation for this is practising trust on a daily basis and engraving trust into the DNA of the enterprise. This is then reflected in the way employees, suppliers, customers, and indeed the whole spectrum of stakeholders, are **treated on a daily basis**. For example, at Amazon, junior employees are trusted to withdraw products from sale if they see a pattern of faults with a particular item. They are not required to fill in time-consuming forms etc. to request that the item is withdrawn.

> *"Employees learn to trust when leaders provide adequate information about decisions they are making."*

> Andy Atkins, Interaction Associates.

In his 2014-15 research, *Building Workplace Trust,* Andy Atkins demonstrates that companies that enjoy high levels of **trust** among **their employees** are two and a half times as likely, than those that don't, to enjoy **superior revenue growth**. So, what should enterprises do to increase the levels of trust across their enterprise? Firstly, in words variously attributed to Mother Teresa, Nun, Missionary and Noble Peace Prize Winner "**Be faithful in small things because it is in them that your strength lies**". People at all levels in organisations **see** what their managers and leaders are doing and even the smallest actions can influence **norms of behaviour**. Secondly, the enhanced focus on integrity, following the great recession of 2008, has highlighted the significance of Leaders and Managers **setting the tone,** at all levels in organisations. Some have labelled this an **Integrity Quotient,** and emphasized the importance of Leaders visibly institutionalizing integrity into the DNA of enterprises. For example, Yuri Rozenfeld, an experienced General Counsel wrote in *Guilty - What's Your Organization's IQ (Integrity Quotient)?*

> *"Creating a truly ethical culture within a company does not happen by itself or by accident. It takes commitment and diligence by the leadership to nurture [and] cultivate these values and behaviors and encourage employees to follow them."*

As with other areas of business activities, appropriate measurement helps achieve and maintain intent. In his World Economic Forum article *3 ways to build trust in your business*[101], Sridharan Nair, the Managing Partner of PwC Malaysia, discusses the PwC research into the question of *"What makes up trust and can it be quantified?"* The following framework emerged from their focus group based research:

---

[101] Nair, S, *3 ways to build trust in your business, World Economic Forum, 30 May 2016.* Available from https://www.weforum.org/agenda/2016/05/3-ways-to-build-trust-in-your-business-05866831-1d47-4d4f-8b16-88ad8e0b7e59/

Figure 47: PWC Trust Framework

Sridharan Nair suggests that organisations should develop measures in 3 areas to keep a focus on key drivers of trust (and communicate these to your stakeholders):

1. **Competence.** For example **on time, on budget, on or above specification**.

2. **Experience**. For example, is the organisation keeping its broader promises. Sridharan Nair uses the example of

customer service in the UK based retailer, Marks and Spencer.

3. Values

"People want brands to understand their needs, to hold the right sort of principles and to care about their impact on society. Clothing retailers that source their cotton from fair trade suppliers are increasingly in demand because they are not seen to be exploiting cheap labour and because their products will benefit small-scale agricultural workers."

Nair (2016)

Moving to **Justness**, I consider this firstly as an **ethical matter**. Even if the ethical argument does not resonate with you, I believe that social media and the increasing **expectations of transparency** will mean that incidents that reflect a **lack of justness** will be **more apparent, more often**. This can be a driver of increased **staff turnover**, damage to **your brand** amongst potential customers and **difficulties with regulators** and other stakeholders.

In his March 2015 TED[102] talk, Paul Tudor Jones II highlighted clearly some **unintended consequences** of a **laser focus on profits.** He suggests that this is "threatening the very underpinnings of society." He talks of the need for a counter-offensive, centred on the concept of

---

[102]

https://www.ted.com/talks/paul_tudor_jones_ii_why_we_need_to_rethink_capitalism,

justness. This starts with business recognising that **inequality** is an issue. To define the criteria for **just corporate behaviour,** Paul Tudor Jones and some friends have started an enterprise named **Just Capital**. This not-for-profit enterprise is gathering public perceptions in a survey of a representative sample of 20,000 Americans. For example, are **living wage jobs, healthy products** and **not harming the environment** public **expectations** that all enterprises should embrace? They are planning to gather the data needed to rank the top 1000 companies in the United States in the form of a **Just Index**[103].

The popularity of *"Capital in the 21st Century",* the surprisingly fast selling 2014 Economics book by Thomas Picardy, is further evidence of increasing interest in inequality. I link this to a concern for justice. When this is combined with increasing **demands for transparency**, I sense growing obligations on enterprises to **communicate more effectively** with all their stakeholders. This needs to include **proactive explanations** of the rationale for contentious actions. For example high Executive Pay settlements or decisions that appear to put profits ahead of concern for social and/or the environment. In practice people's actions are **driven by emotion** at least as much as by rational thought. In their quest to improve the

---

[103] Please see http://justcapital.com for more details.

understanding of human behaviour, Behavioural Economists have developed the **Ultimate Game.**[104] This illustrates what happens when people sense that outcomes are not fair or just. In the game, that has been used in a number of research studies by Richard Thaler and others, the first player is given a sum of money. For the sake of this example, I will assume £1000. The First player is required to give some of this money to the second player. If they agree on the split, they can keep the money; however if the second player disagrees then they both lose all the money. Approaching this from a rational perspective, one could perhaps assume that if the second player is offered £100 they will accept it because they would be £100 better offer than they were before. In repeated iterations of the game, this is not what happens in practice. If the second player feels he or she is being insulted because of the relatively small percentage being offered, they decide to teach the other person a lesson and refuse the £100 so that Player 1 is £900 worse off. The experiments have shown that Player 2 needs to be offered at least 30% in order to secure their acceptance. David Trott argues in his Blog that the feelings of unjustness that drive refusals of offers in the Ultimate Game can explain the results of the

---

[104] Thaler, R.H., *Misbehaving: The Making of Behavioural Economics*, Penguin, 2015

United Kingdom's vote in 2016 to leave the European Union.

"The Brexit vote was the culmination of years of frustration. Those voters felt insulted and ignored. So they behaved like the second player in the ultimatum game. They voted emotionally instead of rationally. If we want to learn it, there's a lesson there for us. We are the urban elite. We live inside an echo chamber. The lesson for those of us in mass media is that we need to stop surrounding ourselves with people who think like us. It will make us lazy, complacent and, worst of all, ineffective."[105]

In the next section I argue for a wide-ranging approach to **setting goals**, so that the needs and wants of a **broad spectrum of stakeholders** are considered, rather than focusing purely on short term **maximisation of shareholder value.**

Beyond Shareholder Value

"ANY organisation - a company, a government ministry, a charity, the local golf club - tends to become inward-looking if there is too little external discipline. Reams of academic literature have been produced to show how civil servants, however good-hearted, naturally act in their own interests, boosting their budgets, protecting their power, resisting outside scrutiny. So it is in private companies, except that managers there face discipline from competition with other firms, from the need to satisfy customers and from the demands of shareholders. Competition and pressure from customers have both become a lot more intense in most

---

[105] http://www.campaignindia.in/article/a-view-from-dave-trott-brexit-and-behavioural-economics/428292

industries in the past two decades, all over the world, with beneficial effects on productivity and innovation."

The Economist (2013)

In the 20 years leading up to the financial crunch in 2008, there was a trend towards focusing on **maximising shareholder value**. More recently I have sensed increasing calls for companies to be **less short term focused** (for example "The Kay Review of UK Equity Markets and Long-Term Decision Making"[106]). Stakeholders (including broader society) is calling for strategies that will deliver **more sustained performance,** (in an environment that increasingly demands **more restrained consumption of natural resources** and a **smaller carbon footprint)**. Incidentally, I sense that dealing effectively with climate change, opens up great business opportunities. The following quote resonates particularly strongly with me:

"I fully encourage companies to maximize the opportunities to mitigate risks, reduce costs, and profit - in both the short term and the long term - by finding solutions to global challenges such as climate change, poverty, education, healthcare, human rights, and ecosystem degradation."

Alice Korngold (2014)

In the United Kingdom, the Institute of Directors is working with the Z/Yen Group and the Cass Business School to develop a **Good Governance**

---

[106] Kay, J., *The Kay Review of UK Equity Markets and Long-Term Decision Making*, Department of Business, Innovation and Skills, July 2012.

Index. *The Great Governance Debate – Towards a Good Governance Index for Listed Companies* (2015), goes well beyond focusing on shareholder value and measuring compliance. It is intended to both stimulate debate around good governance and to contribute to rebuilding the overall **reputation and legitimacy** of the UK business community.

At a strategic level, the current Board Charter initiative in the United Kingdom is focusing attention on actions to help Businesses recognise and deliver **positive impacts on society**. Done effectively, this should help maintain what amounts to **a license to operate**.[107]

> *"The success of our economy depends on well-managed companies with good boards of directors. So, for the success of the economy we need boards which come close to what is in the Charter – the closer they get, the more successful we will be."*
> David Pitt-Watson
> Chair, UN Environmental Programme Finance Initiative and Executive Fellow, London Business School

Away from the United States and United Kingdom, there are perhaps broader traditions of looking beyond shareholders. For example Peter Cappelli, Harbir Singh, Jitendra V. Singh and Michael Useem (2010) have written about the

---

[107] http://www.mazars.co.uk/Home/About-us/Business-in-Society/Business-in-Society-The-Board-Charter

extent to which Indian Managers go beyond shareholder interests to **public mission and national purpose**.

In our increasingly **volatile environments**, I sense that organisations that are engaging effectively with a **broad spectrum of stakeholders** are better able to make effective decisions as circumstances change. For example following the rapid drop in oil prices in the final quarter of 2014, Andrew Hill[108] wrote in the Financial Times of the pricing challenge for managers:

"Francesco Barosi of Alix Partners, the consultancy, says most companies "instead of looking ahead are looking back." Very few are good at both tactical pricing, which depends on managing existing contracts and orders, and strategic pricing, which involves keeping an eye on the horizon. Most ignore even valuable internal information from customers and suppliers that can allow them to anticipate volatility and be less reactive."

In the next section I discuss **managing expectations**, as a foundation for considering practical steps for improving relationships with the spectrum of stakeholders that were identified in at the beginning of this chapter.

---

[108] Financial Times 16 December 2014 – *Oil's decline poses a pricing challenge for managers*, Andrew Hill

Managing Expectations

The first step is to **develop a list** of all the organisations and categories of individuals that have a **stake in your enterprise**. For the sake of discussion in this chapter I will focus on the categories of stakeholders previously mentioned:

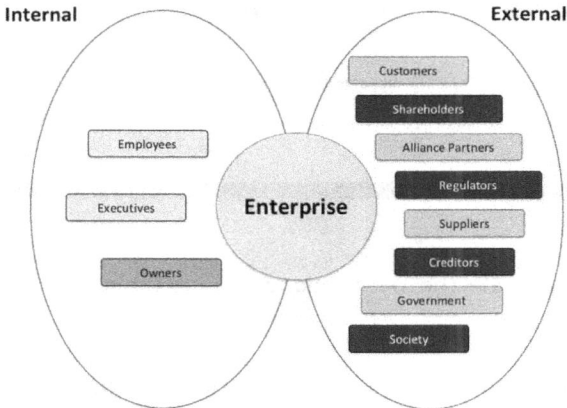

Figure 48: Internal and External Stakeholders

Having identified your Stakeholders, the next step is to consider the **type of relationship** you are aiming to have with **each stakeholder**. For example, you may have a long-term outsourcing arrangement with a supplier that involves real **partnering** that improves performance in ways that **benefit both parties**. On the other hand, you may purchase stationary on a totally transactional basis where every order goes to the cheapest supplier. In these cases I would focus on building engagement with the outsourcing supplier and not invest time and effort building relationships with transactional suppliers.

I suggest that you take a piece of paper and draw a line as shown below. Position each of your main stakeholders on the **Transactional** to **Partnership** continuum, on the basis of the **perception of your enterprise**.

Where are each of your stakeholders on this 'transactional' to 'partnership' continuum?

Transactional   Partnership

Figure 49: The Transactional - Partnership Relationship Continuum

The next step is then to think of your enterprise through the **lens of your stakeholders**. Repeat the exercise so that you have a supplier's perspective of whether the **relationship** with you is a **transactional** one, or one that they consider a **partnership**.

Armed with these insights, view the following graphic and then try **inserting the names** for your **stakeholders** in the appropriate positions.

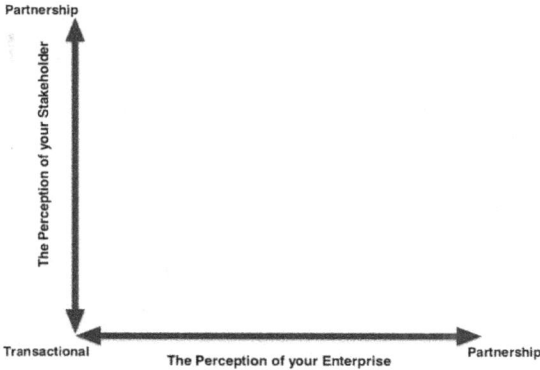

Figure 50: Transactional & Partnership Relationships

If there is shared understanding between your stakeholders and your enterprise of whether a relationship is transactional or a partnership, you have a solid basis for moving forward.

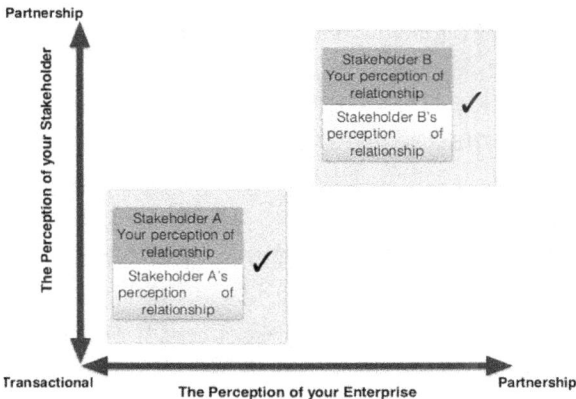

Figure 51: Transactional & Partnership Relationships - 2

On the other hand, if there is a mismatch as shown in the following graphic, there is likely to be continuous stress in the relationship.

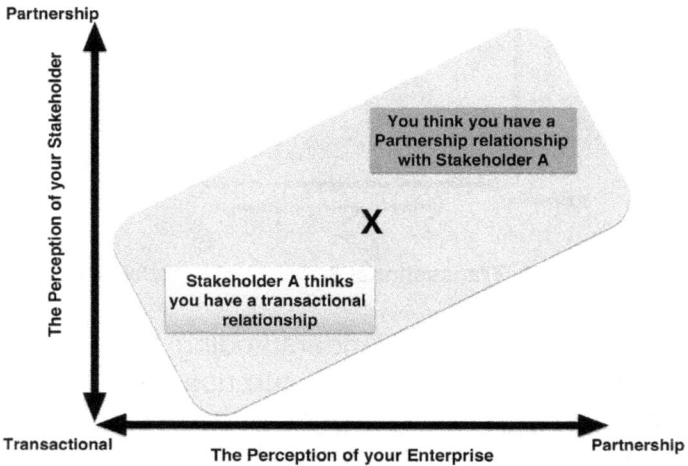

Figure 52: Transactional & Partnership Relationships - 3

Having identified the **stakeholders** that merit **proactive management**, the next step focuses on developing and understanding appropriate expectations. This can avoid tensions and dissatisfaction. For example, Amazon receives criticism over marginal profitability in some sections of the press; however, the company has been very clear in **setting shareholder**

expectations.[109] There should therefore be no surprises about financial performance:

> *"A fundamental measure of our success will be the shareholder value we create over the long term. From the very beginning, our emphasis has been on the long term and as a result, we may make decisions and weigh trade-offs differently than some other companies. Accordingly, it is important for you, our shareholders, to understand our fundamental management and decision-making approach so that you may ensure that it is consistent with your own investment philosophy."*

> Amazon.com Web Site 18 Dec 2014: http://phx.corporate-ir.net/phoenix.zhtml?c=97664&p=irol-govHighlights

In chapter 2 I discussed managing the expectations of your clients and pointed out that I have used the same approach to managing the expectations of my own bosses. I believe that there is value in extending the approach to all **stakeholders of significance**, as a foundation for taking **proactive actions** to engage with each of the key groups. Using the matrix below should help.

---

[109] Bezos, J.P., *1997 Letter to Shareholders*, Amazon.com http://media.corporate-ir.net/media_files/irol/97/97664/reports/Shareholderletter97.pdf

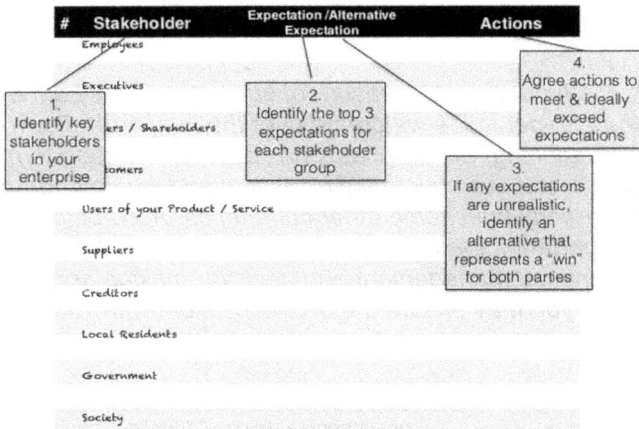

Figure 53: Actions to meet Stakeholder Expectations

The dialogue involved in this process can provide a rich stream of **insights** that can help both **current performance** and your **agility**. Sensing **changes more quickly** in the competitive environment (amongst the chain of stakeholders that create value, and the owners of your enterprise), enables you to be more proactive. This will avoid situations where an **expectation gap** develops. The following example is from a family business where one might have assumed that the risk of such an expectation gap was low.

The enterprise had grown steadily through the 1990s and early 2000's, under the leadership of a CEO who owned 40% of the equity in the business. Members of the CEO's extended family owned the remaining 60% and had shown little, if any interest, in the management of the enterprise. Over the last 20 years, 75% of the profits of the enterprise had been retained and used to fund expansion and pay down debts. The enterprise had minimal borrowings in 2008. Revenues held steady in 2009 and but they were only being maintained in 2010 by introducing discounts. The CEO and his senior managers undertook a comprehensive review of the business and concluded that they should expand geographically into emerging markets in Latin America, where a long standing friend had good contacts from his time as an Attaché in an Embassy in Brazil. The CEO prepared a paper for a Board Meeting outlining the current situation, the review of the enterprise and the conclusion. The CEO was shocked when the board rejected his paper and requested his resignation. Subsequently a new CEO from outside the family was appointed, on an interim basis, and two consultants were engaged to develop a profit improvement programme and options for the sale of the business.

As Paul Polman[110], the CEO of Unilever, recognises, it is important for companies of all sizes to seek to **understand**[111] the **spectrum of**

[110] Polman, P., *Business, Society and the Future of Capitalism*, McKinsey Quarterly, May 2014.
[111] Steven Covey in his book 7 Habits of Effective People (Covey, S.R., *The 7 Habits of Effective People®*, Simon & Schuster UK Ltd.,1989.) emphasizes the principle of seeking to understand a particular issue before then moving the dialogue on to your point of view and your effort "to seek to be understood."

objectives held by their **shareholders**. You can then decide which ones are consistent with the strategic direction, acknowledging that this is likely to result in the **loss of some shareholders**, but hopefully a **stronger relationship** with those that remain. These relationships can be strengthened further as your stakeholder engagement activities improve **stakeholders' understanding** of your **strategic direction**, plans and performance.

"Any company - certainly a company of our size [Unilever]- has thousands if not millions of shareholders, and they can have different objectives. Some want you to spin off businesses and get a quick return. Some want share buybacks, some want dividend increases, some want you to grow faster. It's very difficult to run a company if you try to meet the needs of all your shareholders. So we spent time identifying those we thought would feel comfortable with our longer-term growth model instead of catering to shorter-term interests."

Paul Polman (2014)

I encourage all Leaders to develop a simple **annual plan of activities** to secure, and then optimise **dialogues with stakeholders**. The objective being that **stakeholder engagement** improves year on year and Executives are not faced with a shock like the one outlined above. Moreover, this dialogue should improve the stakeholders' understanding about the enterprise and provide a foundation for improved commitment to the company.

Engaging Stakeholders

"Make no mistake, the keys to surviving and thriving, as individuals and organizations, will not primarily be the 'out of the box' cleverness of our 'strategic response,' but instead individual and organizational character as expressed by the depth and breadth of relationships throughout our individual or organizational networks."

Tom Peters, 6 July Weekly Quote (2015)

In this section I will consider each of the major categories of stakeholder and consider **actions** that can be taken to **improve the effectiveness** of engagement.

Employees

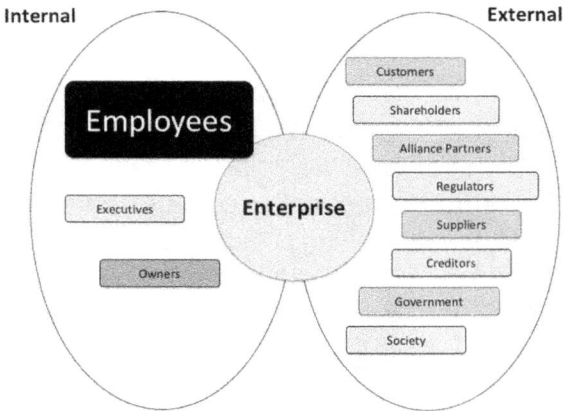

Figure 54: Enterprise Stakeholders

Traction for the activities I have discussed in this book will necessitate securing **discretionary effort** from people. Much is being written about employee engagement and some researchers, such as John Hagel, argue that leading enterprises now need not just engaged people but people who have a real passion for **their work** and for **creating value for customers**.

> *"While much work has been done to understand and improve employee engagement, employee engagement is no longer enough. Times have changed. Worker passion – defined by three attributes [Commitment to Domain and Questing and Connecting dispositions] rather than static skills that rapidly diminish over time – will be critical as we shift from a twentieth century world characterised by scalable efficiency to a twenty-first-century world amplified by scalable learning."*

"Unlocking the passion of the Explorer" John Hagel III, Deloitte University Press 17 Sep 2013.

The **commitment to domain** refers to having an **increasing impact** on a particular industry or component(s) of an enterprise. Individuals with the **questing** attribute actively seek out challenges to improve their capabilities. Another way of looking at this has been articulated by Sir Clive Woodward, the World Cup Winning Coach of the England Rugby Team. He emphasises the importance of individuals having a **thirst for knowledge and learning**, indeed a real passion for their subject. Those with the **connecting**

disposition develop deep interactions with colleagues and the wider world and create **trusting relationships** that enable them to surface **new insights**.

In thinking further about the **purpose - engagement - passion challenge**, I believe that it is important to recognise that the objective is to raise **the level of contribution of all the people in your enterprise** - not just the senior people or the top performers. Two examples I like to quote to illustrate individuals in junior jobs having a sense of purpose are:

- A person on the Kevlar production line for body armour who when asked by Ellen Kullman, the CEO of DuPont, what they were doing answered "Saving lives",
- The man sweeping the floor at NASA, told the then President, that his job was "putting a man on the moon".

To achieve such a strongly engrained sense of purpose we need to coherently **explain how individuals' activities contribute to achieving the Enterprise's vision**. This needs something much more meaningful to an individual than the traditional mission statement.

The challenge then is to **secure optimum business performance**, both **now and in the future**. To achieve this necessitates agile performance that **cultivates customers** that are **more than satisfied** as their **needs evolve**. A key to this in my experience is having people that are truly engaged and passionate about being better than their counterparts in other enterprises (now and in the future).

"Our world has changed and is changing in ways that call for a transformational response from organisations in attitudes and in ways of doing things, especially in ways of leading, managing and organising people"

Janice Caplan (2013)

Promoting a **focus on the future**, as well as today, is a foundation for developing the **commitment** that will drive the **discretionary behaviour** agile enterprises particularly need. Leaders at all levels in the enterprise who **communicate a clear vision**, a **strategic direction that individuals can relate to**, and consistently (and visibly) **live the enterprise values**, create an environment that is much more conducive to having engaged people. In her 2013 Book, Janice Caplan argues persuasively that:

- Business performance improves when people are **engaged** with the organisation.
- The key drivers of employee engagement are those that involve and **empower people**, and provide outstanding opportunity to support and development.

- The recurring theme that enables improved engagement is **open, honest and supportive dialogue**. This includes listening as well as communicating frequently; and that means the bad news as well as the good.

Effective implementation of the ideas outlined in this book necessitates the **involvement of people**. Moreover, **empowered people** that willingly commit discretionary effort, to deliver a much higher level of contribution to **continuous improvement, raising agility and improving stakeholder engagement**.

"Managers and Leaders create the climate for engagement. They have to act in a way that inspire people to think for themselves and do 'whatever it takes' to fulfil the organisational purpose."

Professor Jane McKenzie (2014)

How to build employee engagement?

"Knowing your Talent is as important as knowing your numbers"

Stacy Feiner (2015)

Firstly, a quick win ...... **walk about and talk to your people**, show interest in them and thank them for particular contributions they are making. For this to be effective, it needs to be **sincere and related to very specific actions the individual has taken**. When doing this, and indeed when giving any form of performance feedback, I find it helpful to think about emulating a sports coach. I endeavour to be **very specific** and start by reminding the individual about a specific aspect of their performance (in as an objective way as possible) and then making a specific **suggestion for improving performance** in that specific activity. As Tom Peters (2012) has observed, there is no greater gift to people whom you engage, than a heartfelt (as well as head-felt) acknowledgement of their contribution and fundamental human worth. When these conversations are taking place, during a **period of significant change**, you have a great opening to **explain** the **Big Opportunity** behind the change initiative - as part of creating a sense of urgency for the change.

"It is important that executives keep acknowledging and reinforcing it [the opportunity the change is addressing] so that people will wake up every morning determined to find some action they can take in their day to move toward the opportunity."

John Kotter (2014)

Subsequently, frequent feedback on progress and an honest dialogue about elements of the change that may not be working can help encourage **sustained staff engagement**.

Secondly, promote a concerted effort to institutionalise the identification and development of innovative ideas into your **enterprise DNA**. One tactic that leaders can use is to provide individuals with **top cover** by tolerating new ideas that do not work. Clearly there are limits to this but we need to create **a climate where individuals are not punished for being innovative**. A mechanism I have seen work well (at Andersen Consulting) is to expect that people at all levels **check their thinking** with peers or managers before trying novel approaches. Bear in mind that individuals who are angry with an issue may be difficult to manage, but can be a great engine to power change.[112] It is therefore worth spending time engaging them rather than avoiding them.

Thirdly, **recognise** diversity. Different People have different circumstances, needs & motivators. Actions that are **tuned** to individuals will therefore be the most effective in raising commitment and employee engagement. We should expect that for some people, your enterprise will be the most important thing in their life, for others it will but one of a portfolio of interests.

"When we only try to understand and affect what happens at work, we ignore the most basic tenet of person-organisation fit: employees bring their whole selves to work. What happens after the workday may be just as important as what happens during it."

Susan La Motte

---

[112] Peters, T., "Angry people make Change",
https://www.youtube.com/watch?v=A2EdCl-CX4Q, 2010.

I believe that it is helpful to think about your people in a number of different **dimensions**, as you consider potential actions to improve commitment and engagement. As an aid to better understanding your people consider where you assess each of your key people on the following five dimensions:

1. Length of Service

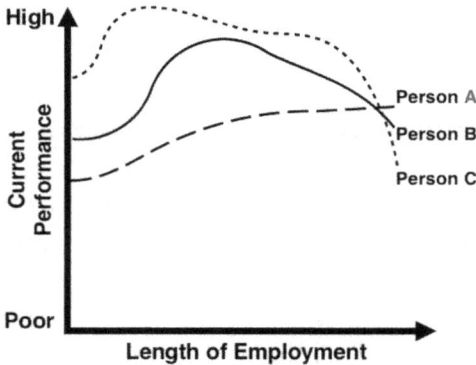

Figure 55: Length of Service

As a gymnastics coach in my youth, a frequent challenge was to help performers rise above **performance plateaus**. This involved a mix of increasing **technical skills** and giving them the **confidence to try new things**. For example adjusting a gymnasts technique so that they achieved more height in a backwards somersault, as a prelude to introducing a twist into the somersault (which would generate the performer more points for difficulty and risk). This was achieved most consistently by taking the performer through a **sequence of development steps** to give them the confidence to **go for it**. A skill was identifying those with the potential to rise above the current performance level and then form a **programme of actions** to exploit that potential. Applying this approach to the talent in your enterprise can start with you identifying **who is operating at a plateau**, but has the **potential to contribute more**? You might like to also think about the gap between each individual's performance and the expectation you had for him or her when they joined your team. Should you consider them for a move to a new role, for a training course to raise their skills, or can you involve them in a special project?

2. *Personal Ambition*

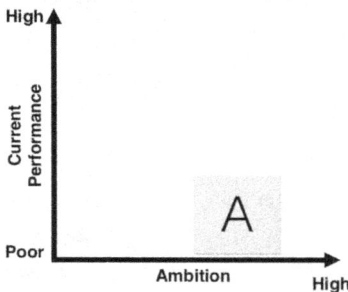

Figure 56: Personal Ambition

Taking this thinking a stage further, consider the level of **ambition** that each employee displays. Then ask whether the individual`s level of ambition is realistic and if so whether it is being adequately **fuelled** by you and your colleagues. Do you have any individuals, in segment A (above), that have particular **development needs?** How can **you help** them to raise their current level of performance, or perhaps **coach** them to better align their **ambition and performance**?

3. *Future Potential*

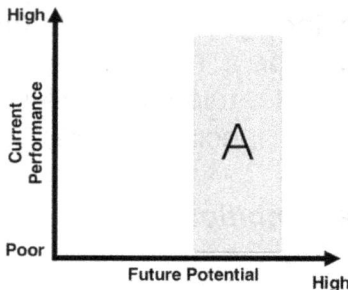

Figure 57: Current Performance v Future Potential

How much **potential** does each person on your team possess? It can be helpful to think of future potential as a combination of **ambition** and a **personal engine** to propel the individual along the journey towards the ambition's destination. Is there a mismatch between current performance and future potential? If there is, how can you help the individual to close the gap? Are the people in Segment A gaining sufficient **personal satisfaction** to be **fully committed** to your enterprise?

4. *Value to the Enterprise*

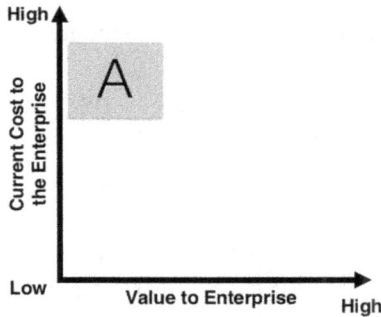

Figure 58: Individual value to the enterprise

Plot a cross section of your people onto this graph. Do you have people in Quadrant A that need a **performance improvement plan** or potentially a move out of your enterprise?

5. *Individual Satisfaction*

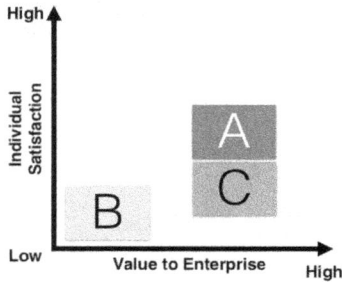

Figure 59: Individual satisfaction v Value

Do you have people who are **contributing great value** to your organisation that are not gaining **individual satisfaction** from their work? Those who are in the area shown as Box C in the graph are at particular risk of moving to new employment, because they **feel** the benefit of **some satisfaction**. You might like to consider special projects or **other responsibilities** for people in this category, to raise their level of satisfaction. It would also be prudent to consider, as a matter of priority, **succession plans** for people in this group, and for those in category A. Finally consider what impact people in category B are having on the rest of your employees and seriously consider whether they have a future in your enterprise. If they do not, how can they be given opportunities to leave your enterprise with dignity?

Next Steps:

Develop a **meaningful dialogue** with each of the people you are directly responsible for. This can flow from:

- The insights on your people that you have gained, including their interests and commitments away from work.
- Your understanding of your enterprise strategy, and in particular, the strategic themes driving your goals and objectives. What does this mean for the behaviours needed from your people? Developing Strategic Themes was an area of focus in the last chapter.
- Your personal point of view on how the people in your enterprise can and should develop their personal capabilities.

If you have uncertainties about the potential of your Managers and Directors, I suggest that you consider using a diagnostic such as Pinsight[113] . This assesses individuals, using a business simulation, in relation to business imperatives that you identify. For

---

[113] https://pinsight.biz/blog/12/pinsight-raises-700-000-funds-to-debut-revolutionary-talent-management-technology/

example, **Increase Customer Satisfaction by improved Customer Service** or **Align the Team with Organisational Strategy**. In his New Year 2015 Blog[114], Martin Lanik the CEO of Pinsight, emphasises the importance of deliberate practice and I believe that this applies to both Leaders and followers.

"Deliberately practicing few very specific exercises is the key to building habits and showing visible improvement. The same way personal trainers target specific exercises to isolated muscle groups, you can build exercises that target specific skills of employees. When a manager needs to better empower her team, she could first practice asking questions instead of giving advice."

The aim should be to agree both **personal commitments** to the enterprise and **enterprise commitments** to the individual, that **align** as far as possible with the needs of both parties. The **shared understanding** developed in this process can then provide a launch pad for improved commitment and performance - and move people up the **commitment ladder**. In an ideal world, these would form the basis of:

1. A **personal development plan.**

---

[114]https://pinsight.biz/blog/11/development-plans-are-like-new-year-s-resolutions-good-on-paper-bad-in-practice-build-habits-instead/

2. An entry in a **readily accessible system** to ensure that the individual's interests are visible when decisions are being made on appointments, or the staffing of initiatives.

As Carol Walker wrote in her 16 September 2015 Harvard Business Review Blog:

"... assigning work should be a thoughtful process that balances business goals with an individual's interest, skills, and development needs. Not every routine task has to be so thoroughly considered. But whenever significant assignments are made, putting them into context maximizes their impact. An employee who understands why she has been asked to do something is far more likely to assume true ownership for the assignment."

Approaches such as this can help promote **proactive management** of the talent you have in your enterprise. This should help you achieve the win-win-win, of **better achievement** of enterprise goals, more **satisfied people** and better **development of the capabilities** needed for future success. For example if you have noted that the accuracy of your sales forecasts is being degraded as a result of one individual, this person's development plan could usefully include coaching / training[115] on how to develop better assumptions for their forecasts.

---

[115] Lunn, B., "Mindshare to Marketshare", Amazon, 2014.

"Great leadership is about creating a free and open conversation within a framework of shared values, share visions and shared understanding."

Janice Caplan (2013)

The Times 100 Business Case Studies includes an example of the approach to talent management used at Siemens. This achieves these outcomes by **developing people** and **matching** them to the tasks needed to realise the **Siemens vision**. The Siemens' talent management philosophy involves making sure that **every employee** is provided with the **guidance and support** needed to achieve their full potential (not just the high flyers).

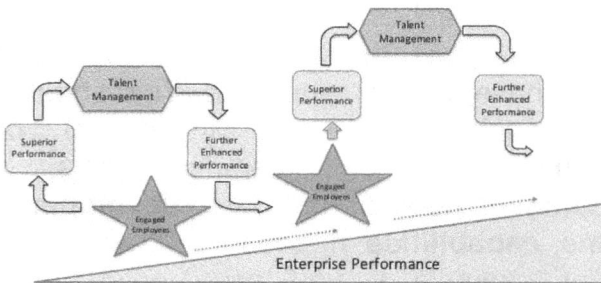

Figure 60: Talent management cycle

The outcome of the process is **transparency** between the **enterprise strategy** and the **talent development plans** for each individual. **Targets** relevant to the role and responsibilities are **cascaded** to each individual. Through meeting these personal targets each **individual optimises** their contribution to the **achievement** of overall **enterprise targets**. Individuals are consequently clear about the impact of their performance and the consequences for their own development. The information collected during this process, **owned** and updated by the individual concerned, is recorded in an enterprise system. When **roles need to be filled**, the enterprise system can then be queried to produce a list of **people** that have the **potential** and **interest** for the role. In leading edge enterprises these enterprise systems are a lot more than a documentation of annual performance reviews. Organisations such as Accenture, Deloitte and GE now expect **regular, meaningful, feedback** to be provided as a standard part of managing the business. Smartphone applications are being introduced to help avoid this becoming an overly administrative chore.

What works well for Siemens will not work elsewhere if the processes are not appropriate to your particular **business context**, or consistent with the **perspectives** of enterprise **leadership**. As Stacy Feiner (2015) points out in *"Talent Mindset: The Business Owner's Guide to Building Bench Strength"*, people processes from one enterprise (particularly a large one), do not invariably work in another enterprise (particularly a smaller one).

"We took pieces and parts out of context from GE's talent management story, and hoped for the best. With 20/20 vision, we now realize the essential lesson to learn is that each CEO must evolve their own unique philosophy from which a unique set of unequivocal expectations are born, and ultimately executed with necessary passion and conviction."

Customers

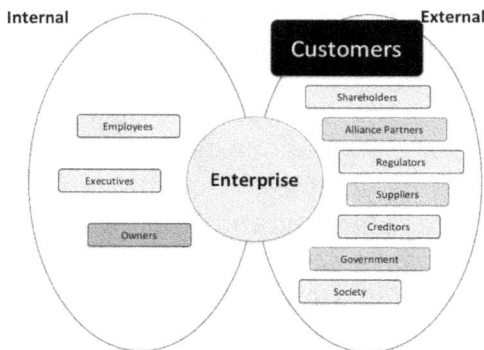

"...Companies that make their customer partners, and share the value created, lead the pack on revenue growth, profit margins, capital efficiency and enterprise value."

Libert et al (2015)

For years some companies have provided **some customers** with the **capability to customise** some products to their specific needs. For example, Trek bicycles, M&M

sweets, Nike running shoes and Dell computers. Indeed one might view this as turning the clock back to the time when goods were manufactured for a specific customer. In their July 2015 Harvard Business School article, Barry Libert, Yoram (Jerry) Wind, and Megan Beck Fenley argue that digital technologies are enabling companies such as Apple, AirBnB and Lending Club to go much further in **tuning** their offerings. Expanding **digital technologies** enable **new value chains,** where partnering entities jointly create value, by **innovating across company boundaries**. These companies successfully orchestrate value-creating activities across their network. This is supported by arrangements to share assets, knowledge and stakeholder relationship in exchange for a share of revenues and profits. For example Amazon provides design, manufacturing, distribution and accounting services for authors who share their knowledge (in books they have written). **Both parties** then **share the revenues** from book sales. One should expect this business model to become more and more widespread. Now I would like you to reflect on two questions:

1. How could your enterprise benefit from partnering in this way?

2. Who could emerge as a competitive threat and threaten your revenues and profit.

Shareholders

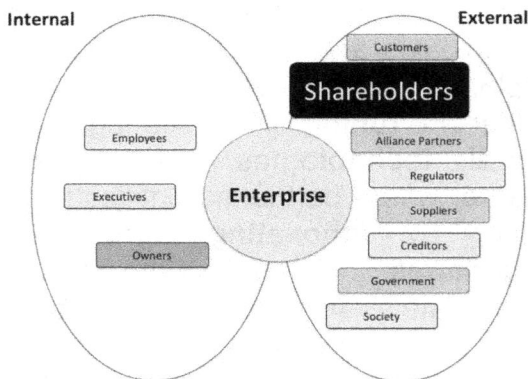

This section is intended to provide an outline of considerations for **managing relations** with shareholders at small and medium sized companies that are too small to have investment relations departments or specialist staff.

This brief discussion will draw on both thinking developed for larger companies, such as the UK Financial Reporting Council's *Stewardship Code* and initiatives such as the UK Institute of Directors (IOD) work with ecoDA to develop a governance agenda for unlisted companies in the UK. The focus is on

actions for private enterprises that are not subject to stock exchange listing rules or the Corporate Governance codes intended for larger companies.

The foundation for relations between shareholders and a company should be a constitutional and **governance framework,** that reflects the current activities of the company. A good start point on considering shareholder engagement is therefore a review to establish whether the constitution and governance framework is **fit for purpose**. I have seen too many examples of companies that have not updated these to reflect the evolution of their enterprise.

One of the principles articulated in *Corporate Governance Guidance and Principles for Unlisted Companies in the UK* published by IOD/ecoDa is particularly relevant to this discussion:

1. There should be a dialogue between the board and the shareholders based on a mutual understanding of objectives. The board as a whole has responsibility for ensuring that a satisfactory dialogue with shareholders takes place. The board should not forget that all shareholders should be treated equally.

2. This responsibility formally resides with the Chairman of the Board and should be viewed as a continuous process rather than confined to an Annual General Meeting (assuming that you have one)[116].

The nature and the **diversity of the shareholder population** will influence the most practical and **efficient approach** companies use to engage with **their shareholders**. Recently I attended an enjoyable informal evening that **Justpark**[117] held for their shareholders. This enabled me to talk to a cross section of their staff and gain a better **understanding** of their **organisational culture**. Moreover, the company has engaged Shareholders in searching for unused space that could be used for additional car parking that can be rented through the https://www.justpark.com. For some companies Shareholder newsletters have been the traditional vehicles for communication, notwithstanding the limitations of one-way communication.

I encourage you to think about how **new technology** could enable a **more effective dialogue** with your shareholders, in a cost effective way. Could for example, Twitter's

---

[116] Unlisted companies in the UK are not required to hold Annual General Meetings.
[117] https://www.justpark.com

Periscope software application[118] be used to give your Shareholders a **view of your day-to-day activities** on their Smartphones? This could open up a dialogue with your Shareholders that could identify new business opportunities as well as improving Shareholder **loyalty**.

The relatively illiquid market for unlisted company shares can be a powerful incentive for shareholders in these entities to engage in discussions with company boards. On the other hand, some companies have a material number of shareholders who own shares for only short periods (in some cases only fractions of a second, where high frequency trading is being used). Reviewing **who owns your shares** is valuable, as is establishing a mechanism for alerting Executives to any significant purchases or sales of shares.

---

[118] https://www.periscope.tv

Alliance Partners

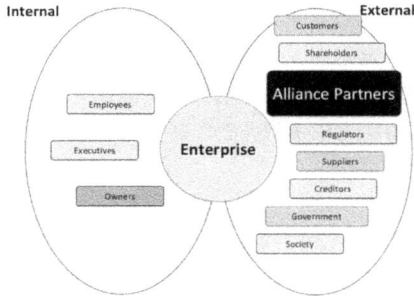

In some industries strategies that involve using a spectrum of alliance partners to expand the reach of an enterprise have been very successful. For example SAP, the large German software company uses a network of partnerships to extend the penetration of their software products across the world. This includes [119]:

- Alliances with enterprises such as large global consulting firms,
- Original equipment manufacturers who integrate SAP with their own products and may bundle or host SAP with other software,
- Solution providers who provide "added value" by combining their business,

---

[119] An example used by Slack, Nigel, Alistair Brandon-Jones, Robert Johnston in *Operations Management, 7th Edition.* Pearson Higher Education (UK).

technical or application expertise with SAP software,

- Complementary technology partners that provide software solutions that extend and add value to the standard SAP solutions,
- Volume resellers who earn license fees by selling all or part of the SAP software portfolio,
- Authorized education partners who are authorized by SAP to provide official training to ensure that customers' employees gain optimal training.

Other companies may use alliance partners to deliver physical products, or to enable a broader range of services to be provided to their clients. For example, one of the big 4 Global Professional Services Partnerships engages me to provide strategy and planning workshops for their clients in the Middle East. Such partner strategies are also viable for much smaller enterprises. Indeed, some start-ups build their business on the basis of being a channel partner for a larger established business (albeit that this can involve its own risks).

In all these cases, enduring relationships necessitate an **understanding of the expectations** of the respective parties and a recognition that both parties will need to **secure continuing value** from the arrangement. Most value will be added when **trust** is developed between the parties to the point where details of

future plans are shared and value adding capabilities from both parties are built into future products.

In our ever more agile, ever more complex world, I expect companies to increasingly use alliance partners to both extend the range of products offered, and the spectrum of clients served. Managing these relationships successfully will necessitate enterprises developing their management skills. Research into the workstyles of successful partner managers [120] identified the following work style characteristics amongst successful partner managers:

- *"Ability to lead and influence,*
- *Willingness to take initiative with little or no supervision,*
- *Strategic/global thinkers seeking and creating opportunities,*
- *Capable of dealing with high levels of ambiguity,*
- *Highly innovative, dynamic, creative, independent thinkers,*
- *People-oriented with high empathy,*
- *Highly cooperative, preferring to work in teams,*
- *Effective at networking across organizational boundaries,*

---

[120] http://phoenixcg.com/files/Strategic%20Leaders.pdf

- *Apt to flex rules to get things done (likely to suffer in bureaucratic environments)."*

I believe that **Coaching** these capabilities will not only improve alliance management, but also individuals Leadership potential and strengthen your pipeline of future senior executives.

Government and Regulators

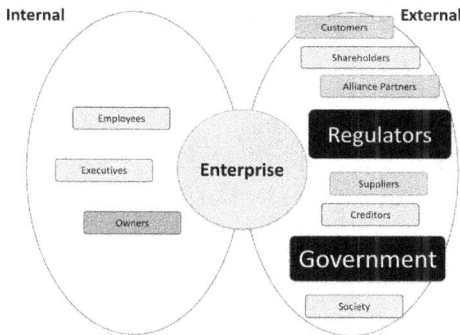

Government significantly impacts the context for how we compete through, for example, company, employment and tax law in the countries in which we choose to operate.

Changes in regulation may create **new opportunities** (for example the changing of rules for banking licenses in the UK) or add dramatically to our costs (for example the requirement to ring fence retail banks in the UK).

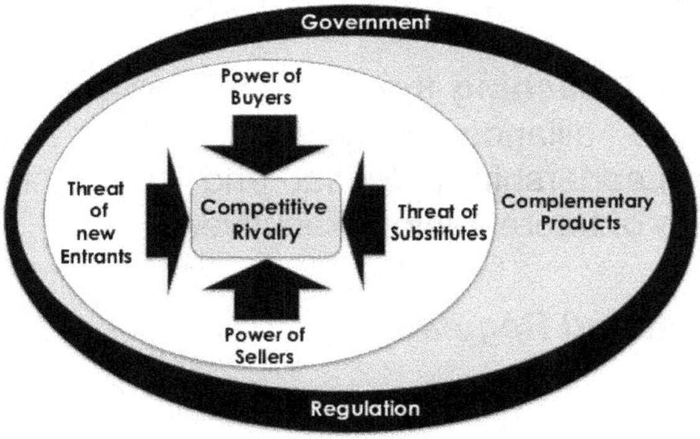

Figure 61: 7 Forces impacting competition

Enterprises can legitimately influence such changes, by taking an active role in government or regulators consultations. Seeking to influence policy through organisations such as the institute of Directors and the Confederation of British Industry in the United Kingdom can be cost effective approach. I believe that enterprises, of all sizes, should invest some time and effort in communicating their point of view on key business issues. In the process you are likely to strengthen your network and raise awareness of potential opportunities (and indeed threats), earlier, so that you have more time to react.

At a local level, are you alert to potential changes in the use of the property and land around your enterprise? For example if there is a proposal to change the use of the building next to you from office space to a bar or restaurant, you may have concerns for the impact on your working environment. In this case it would be valuable to investigate arguments you could use with the organisation responsible for regulation of property use in your area.

Suppliers

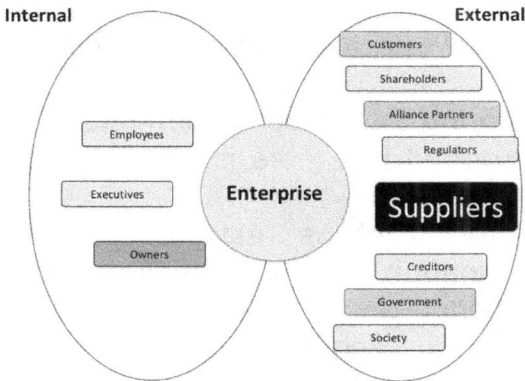

Make of buy is a strategic question that I sense is becoming increasingly important in our world of intense global competition. The **digitisation** of management information, the Internet and cheaper, more efficient global distribution, provides **new opportunities for companies to specialise**.

Enterprises now have greater potential to **focus** on the elements of a **value chain** where they have the most **comparative and**

competitive advantage. They then buy in the rest of the services or products they need to meet their customer needs.

Following the **make or buy** decision, enterprises should consider whether to develop very **close relationships** with a **small number** of **suppliers,** or operate on a **transactional basis** with a **larger pool** of suppliers. Benefits from close cooperation with a small number of selected suppliers can include:

- **Sharing** the economic **benefits** of success (provided that there is full transparency of information),
- Once **trust** is established, joint **co-ordination of activities** so that opportunities for comparative advantage are maximised,
- More **effective problem solving**, and indeed **learning**, from the greater **pool of expertise**.

Debtors and Creditors

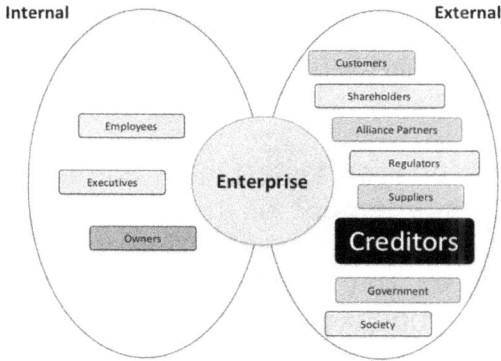

For those who have no experience of accounting, a debtor is a person or enterprise that owes money to another entity or person. The person or entity owed the money, for example a supplier or, a bank is the creditor.

When making new sales do you make a **conscious decision** about the **credit terms** you are including with your product or service? For example, you may insist on payment in advance, perhaps via a credit card on a web site or through a call centre. Where your product or service involves deferred payment do you:

- Validate the client's credit worthiness before finalising the sale?
- Monitor the timely receipt of payments from your clients?

- Take prompt action to encourage rapid payment of monies that are overdue?
- Use the actual payment patterns of your clients as assumptions in your cash flow forecasts?

In periods of faster than normal growth, **close management** of the above points can be vital to ensuring that you have the **funds needed to pay your bills**. Moreover, the approach you take to paying bills and securing payments from your customers is a **foundation for your business relationships**. A practical illustration of your corporate values.

Society

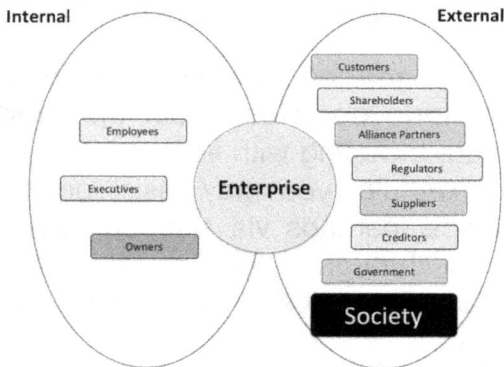

" *Business is here to serve society. We need to find a way to do so in a sustainable and more equitable way not only with resources but also with business models that are sustainable and generate reasonable returns. Take the issues of small-hold farming, food security, and deforestation. They often*

require ten-year plans to address. But if you're in a company like ours [Unilever] and you don't tackle these issues, you'll end up not being in business. We need to be part of the solution. Business simply can't be a bystander in a system that gives it life in the first place. We have to take responsibility, and that requires more long-term thinking about our business model."

Paul Polman 2014

"The businessman is only tolerable so long as his gains can be held to bear some relation to what, roughly and in some sense, his activities have contributed to society."

JM Keynes 1923 [121]

The two quotes above indicate that the topic of business and society is more than a reaction to the great recession of 2008. Rousseau[122] articulated a **social contract**, more than two centuries ago that alerted political leaders that their own **legitimacy would be undermined** if they did not serve the public good. I believe that everyone engaged in business has a responsibility to communicate in ways that go beyond pure marketing. Business people have an obligation to raise society's **understanding of business** so that the legitimacy of business is not increasingly questioned. In order to provide a focus for quantifying the broader costs and benefits of an enterprise to society (including social and ecological considerations), some organisations advocate applying a **triple bottom line** concept.

---

[121] Quoted in *Keynes and Capitalism*, Roger E. Backhouse and Bradley W. Bateman, History of Political Economy, 2009
[122] https://en.wikipedia.org/wiki/The_Social_Contract

This promotes attention to the **impact** of the enterprise on **people, planet and profit.**[123]

For large companies, including **society expectations** as inputs into their **strategy process** can be a transparent way of giving them business importance. The challenge then, in the words of Ian Davis (2005), is to *"articulate business's social contribution and define its ultimate purpose in a way that has more subtlety than "the business of business is business" worldview [Milton Freidman] and is less defensive than most current CSR [Corporate Social Responsibility] approaches."*

Corporate Social Responsibility is a topic that justifies far more discussion than is appropriate to the scope of this book. I would however urge directors and managers to put in place a programme of **actions to engage** with more of society than routine business processes dictate. Such a programme need not be overwhelming if the scope is appropriate to the size and nature of the enterprise. Consider how you can use your **enterprise's skills and resources** in ways that could contribute significantly to **those in need**, at **little cost** to yourselves? Expertise, space, equipment and web-presence can all benefit the

---

[123] Further information can be read at
http://www.investopedia.com/terms/c/corp-social-responsibility.asp#ixzz3lobWVJNX

community. For example businesses of all sizes can:

- Engage with local schools and colleges to help develop an understanding of business.
- Support events organised by Chambers of Commerce, the Institute of Directors, Rotary Clubs and Roundtables etc.
- Host a charity website within your corporate website infrastructure.
- Encourage staff to contribute time to local charities.

Record the progress you make against your plan and also any other CSR activity that your staff may be engaged in as part of their workdays. This can then be **shared with your stakeholders** and may provoke ideas that will both help your business directly and the future programme of your CSR activities. Bear in mind, that by championing the causes you support as you communicate your own CST achievements, you can create a WIN-WIN for both parties.

Finally a quote from a publication from the Institute of Chartered Accountants in Scotland:

"Companies need to shout about the positive things they are doing. Too often they are invisible and seen only on the

defensive when something has gone wrong, when they are portrayed in the media as villains."[124]

David Woods, ICAS Executive Director

Collaboration

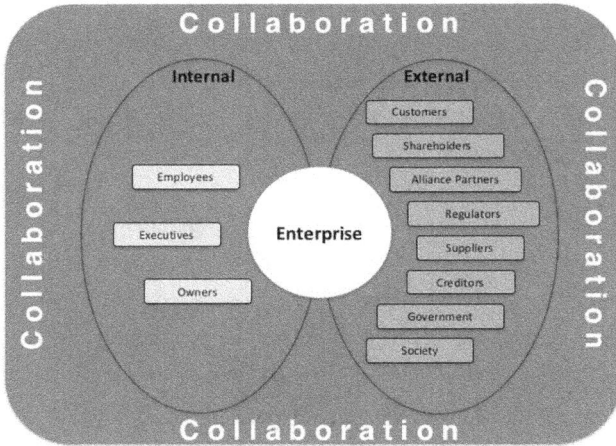

Figure 62: Collaboration across stakeholders

Vineet Nayer argued in a 2014 HBR Blog that a clear sense of purpose and clear goals drives collaboration.

"The next time you want people to collaborate, ask yourself: What is the longing - the deeply felt longing - that will drive this team even if it does not already have all the tools to achieve it? What will wake up the members of the team

---

[124] Available from https://www.icas.com/news/doing-the-right-thing?dm_i=HTX,3HTAF,2IJMB8,CIMTN,1#

every day and make them want to go where they are dreaming of going? When you, as a leader, can articulate that longing and inculcate purpose, you will be well on your way to fostering collaboration among the people in your organization."

The **strategic diamond** that I have previously described promotes a line of sight from purpose through strategic themes to initiatives, measures and targets. I find it particularly helpful to consider the **implications of measures and targets** being discussed for the elements higher up the diamond. This same approach can be used effectively with stakeholders for a specific activity.

Figure 63: Efficienarta Strategic Diamond

I will conclude this chapter with an example of an enduring collaboration between two well-known companies - Apple and Microsoft. The initial relationship was formed because the early Apple Computer used a version of the BASIC programming language that lacked the floating point functionality embedded in the Microsoft version. Subsequently Microsoft developed applications such as Word and Excel especially for Apple, even though at the time Microsoft was focused on the Operating system. At that time the most popular applications were produced by specialists/ For example Lotus 123 (spread sheet) and WordPerfect (word processor). This started a relationship that involved both **collaboration** in some areas and **intense competition** in others.

Turning now to the present, in his Financial Times article, *"The pitfalls of the Microsoft and Apple 'frenemy[125] pact"*, Andrew Hill (2015), highlighted the involvement of a senior Microsoft executive on the stage at a recent Apple product launch. I see this as a return to the old Apple Microsoft collaboration on applications, after a few years of Microsoft exploring alternatives in the Tablet section of the market. Hill, on the other hand, cautions that "friendliness between big companies is only an email away from being a barrier to entry.... An enemy's frenemy is almost certainly not their friend" .... That said he also

---

[125] Sir Martin Sorrell, the CEO of WPP used the term "Frenemy" in 2006 to describe Google as he considered it an example of a company was that both useful to WPP, so a friend, but also a threat to established sources of WPP revenues and profitability.

acknowledged that **frenemy**[126] **is spreading**, quoting, Amazon's new use of the Tmall website operated by Alibaba to reach more customers in China.

Such collaboration however needs on going investment. As Toyota are demonstrating, closer collaboration with suppliers can necessitate **material investment in systems**. Their enhancement of the legendary Toyota Production System, dubbed Toyota New Global Architecture, can both reduce costs and speed time to market. In his 4 June 2015 Financial Times article, Kana Inagaki points out that Toyota's:

> *"attempt to create a "new global architecture" dubbed TNGA — hinges largely on whether its parts makers, some of which are wholly-owned by Toyota, can become more globally competitive."*

I will finish this section with a question:

How can you enhance collaboration with your suppliers?

---

[126] A person or organisation who is a friend in some contexts and a competitive enemy in other situations.

Future Shape of the Winner™

"Peeling the onion with this model highlights what steps are needed to sustain a workforce in today's new realities without shirking from the highest goal of excellence. It creates a freedom to go and do it."

Sales Manager,
Education Services Company, USA

In the last chapter I described the 7S framework that became widely used after it was included in the management classic, *In Search of Excellence,* authored by Peters and Waterman in 1982.

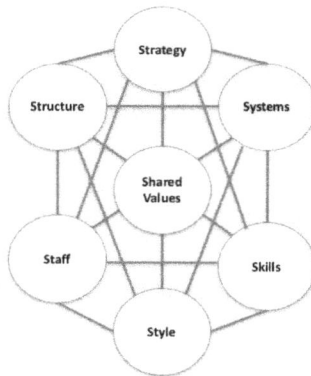

Figure 64: McKinsey 7S Framework

The underlying thinking emphasises that **effective enterprises are a consequence of more than purely great strategy and appropriate structure.** For example, an enterprise with **strong shared-values** in its DNA can be expected to be better able to make **effective decisions** at more **junior levels**. This reduces the burden on the senior leaders who have limited capacity to process the increasing volume of information available in most enterprises.

Tom Peters subsequently developed his Excellence thinking further. This is now embedded in the Future Shape of the Winner™ and Excellence Audit™.

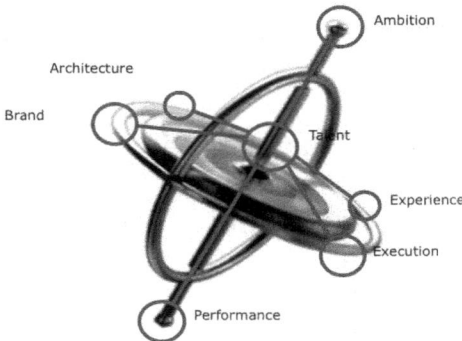

Figure 65: The Tom Peters Company Future Shape of the Winner ™

The use of a gyroscope recognises the combination of **dynamic forces** in an enterprise that interact constantly to find a natural balance, as the enterprise strives to achieve its desired outcomes. For example:

- The experience that customers feel as the **talent in the enterprise brings the brand to life**.
- The **architecture the enterprise evolves** to support the execution of the services and products your customers experience.

Inherent in the approach is a balance of **systems plus passion** (a foundation of the Tom Peters's client work over 30 years). It includes fresh insights, flexibility and practicality to help enterprises **address** the **intense demands** of our ever more **agile** and **resource constrained** world. It considers excellence across 3 axes:

Performance	Experience	Execution
How well are the enterprise's people performing in relation to achieving the enterprise's ambition?	What do your customers experience when in dialogue with your enterprise?	How can leaders enable their talent to deliver the highest quality work output that they can?

Enterprises, in a spectrum of industries from manufacturing to financial services, have used the audit to help form **improvement agendas**. The Enterprises involved have faced a variety of situations including relocation of manufacturing, new services businesses and enterprises that have concluded that they cannot cost cut their way to success. Use of the Audit has helped **galvanise the leadership teams**, around a new agenda. Moreover, insights from an Excellence Audit™ have helped Leadership Teams **understand why** some of their **change programmes** are **running well**, while others are **a source of frustration**.

This **involvement of people** in identifying the priorities for action is another example of how Leaders can practically **enhance employee engagement.** BUT only if they **act on the audit report**! One approach to doing this is to **form project teams,** led by individuals who are considered to have potential to be next generation leaders. They can address the **highest priority capabilities** by developing actions to **close the gaps** between current performance, and the levels identified as necessary in future. These should include measures to obtain and maintain visible, ongoing, top management sponsorship.

5 Conclusions

I encourage you to **engage** all your **stakeholders** in:

- **identifying continuous improvement** opportunities,
- **changes in your competitive environment,**
- **consequent modifications** needed to your enterprise's strategy, structure, systems, staff, skills, style and shared values.

Embedding this involvement **into your "enterprise DNA"** will serve as a robust foundation for developing the enterprise capability you need for a more sustainable future. Moreover,

I believe that this will provide a basis **for raising the engagement of your employees**, and through them, your overall operational excellence and enterprise agility.

"People are proud to work on something where they actually make a difference in life, and that is obviously the hallmark of a purpose-driven business model. We're getting more energy out of the organization, and that willingness to go the extra mile often makes the difference between a good company and a great one."

Paul Polman[127]

I encourage all readers to use the techniques in this book to improve the robustness of the governance of their enterprise by:

1. focusing more attention on recognizing threats,
2. agreeing priorities for relevant actions to address the threats,
3. mobilising the resources required to mitigate the threats and exploit consequent opportunities.

Finally, a quotation that I believe articulates most clearly a sense of ambition that addresses the themes in this book.

---

[127] Polman, P., "Business, Society and the Future of Capitalism", McKinsey Quarterly, May 2014.

Excellence demands we define a path of continuous improvement, constantly challenging existing processes. It also requires us to embrace change so we are in the right place when new opportunities open up. Excellence also means attracting the best talent in the marketplace and giving them the skills and opportunities they need to become high-achievers. We are committed to living a high-performance culture.

Siemens Website February 2014

HUW MORRIS

6 Bibliography

Almquist, A, Senior, J., Bloch, N., "The Elements of Value", Harvard Business Review, September 2016.

American Management Association, Society of Human Resource Management, and the Association of Strategic Alliance Professionals . Today's Alliance Professional...Tomorrow's Strategic Leader, 2009.

Ashcroft, J, "Dimensions of Strategy": http://www.dimensionsofstrategy.com/five-dimensions.html

Ashkenas, R, "Even Good Employees Hoard Great Ideas", HBR Blog, http://blogs.hbr.org/2014/04/even-good-employees-hoard-great-ideas/, 21 April 2014.

Campbell A., "Winners and How they Succeed" Hutchinson, Randon House, 2015.

Chandler, Alfred D., "Strategy and Structure: Chapters in the History of the American Industrial Enterprise", 1962.

Christensen, C.M., "The Clayton M. Christensen Reader", Harvard Business School Publishing Corporation, 2016.

Downes, L., Nunes, P., "Big Bang Disruption: Business Survival in the Age of Constant Innovation", 2014.

Duhigg, C., "Smarter faster better", William Heinemann, London, 2016.

Dunbar, R.I.H., "Coevolution of neocortical size, group size and language in humans", Behavioral and Brain Sciences, 16, pp 681-694 doi:10.1017/S0140525X00032325, 1993.

Edelman Trust Barometer http://www.edelman.com/insights/intellectual-property/trust-2013/, 2013.

Elkington , J., "Cannibals with Forks: Triple Bottom Line of 21st Century Business", Capstone, Oxford, 1997.

Feiner, S., "Talent Mindset: The Business Owner's Guide to Building Bench Strength", Feiner Consulting LLC, 2015.

Ferguson, N., "The Great Degeneration", Penguin Books, 2013.

Financial Times, "Idea Management Software Boosts Collaboration", http://www.ft.com/cms/s/0/c334c148-cada-11e3-9c6a-00144feabdc0.html , 23 April 2014.

Financial Times, "Léo Apotheker: A new life with Europe's stalled Tech groups", http://www.ft.com/cms/s/0/e41a31dc-545e-11e4-84c6-00144feab7de.html?siteedition=intl#axzz3HzRWFwPz , 27 October 2014.

Financial Times, "Azeem Azhar: The company man belongs in the past", 19 May 2016.

Folkman, J., "8 Ways to ensure that your vision is valued", http://www.forbes.com/sites/joefolkman, 22 April 2014.

Forbes, "Forbes Insights Study - Making the Change – Planning, Executing and Measuring Successful Business Transformation", Forbes, 2014.

Ghoshal, S., Barlett, C.A., *Linking organizational context and managerial action: The dimensions of quality of management*, 1994.

Grove, A.S., "Only the Paranoid Survive: How to Exploit the Crisis Points that Challenge Every Company and Career", Broadway Business, 1996.

Harford, T., "The Meaning of Trust in the age of Airbnb", The Financial Times, 10 August 2016.

Hemingway, E., "Fiesta: The Sun also Rises", Jonathan Cape Ltd., 1927.

Hilton, S., "More Human - Designing a World Where People Come First", WH Allen, 2015.

Hossain, M., Development of Statistical Quality Control: Evolution or Revolution, University of North Texas: http://www.academia.edu/2457002/DEVELOPMENT_OF _STATISTICAL_QUALITY_CONTROL_EVOLUTION_O R_REVOLUTION

Kay, J., "The Kay Review of UK Equity Markets and Long-Term Decision Making", Department of Business, Innovation and Skills, July 2012.

Koch, R., Lockwood. G., "Simplify: How the Best Businesses in the World Succeed", Piatkus, London, 2016

Korngold, A., "A Better World, Inc.: How Companies Profit by Solving Global Problems...Where Governments Cannot", Palgrave Macmillan, 2014.

Kotter, J.P, "Accelerate – How the most innovative capitalize on today's rapid-fire strategic challenges and still make their numbers", Harvard Business Review, November 2012.

Kotter, J.P., "Forget the Strategy PowerPoint", HBR Blog Network, 22 April 2014.

Kotter, J.P. , "Accelerate", Harvard Business Review Press, 2014.

Laureani, A., Jiju, A. Douglass, A., "Lean six sigma in a call centre: a case study", International Journal of Productivity and Performance Management, 59(8): http://strthprints.strath.ac.uk/35374

Litan, R.E., "Economists: Don't leave home without one", McKinsey Quarterly, April 2015.

Lunn, B., "Mindshare to Marketshare", Amazon, 2014.

Marr, B., "Big Data – Using Smart Big Data Analytics and metrics to make better decisions and improve performance", Willey, 2015.

McGinn, D., "The Numbers in Jeff Bezos's Head", Harvard Business Review, November 2014.

Moore. D., & Haran, U., "A Simple Tool for Making Better Forecasts", HBR Blog, 19 May 2014.

Morris, H., "Strattomics – Strategies and tactics for an agile world", Amazon, 2014.

Morris, H., "Strattomics – Building Stakeholder Engagement", iBooks Store, 2015.

Nair, S, "3 ways to build trust in your business", World Economic Forum, 30 May 2016.

Peters, T., Watermann, R., "In Search of Excellence", Harper & Row, 1982.

Peters, T, Phillips, J. Watermann. R, "Structure is not Organization", Business Horizons, June 1980.

Peters, T., "Angry people make Change", https://www.youtube.com/watch?v=A2EdCl-CX4Q, 2010.

Peters, T., "A Brief History of the 7S [Mckinsey 7-S] Model, http://tompeters.com/2011/03/a-brief-history-of-the-7-s-mckinsey-7-s-model/, 2011.

Peters, T., "You Matter to Me", IBooks Store, https://itunes.apple.com/us/book/you-matter-to-me/id571283661?mt=11, 2012.

Pettigrew, Andrew M, "The Politics of organizational decision-making", 1973.

Polman, P., "Business, Society and the Future of Capitalism", http://www.mckinsey.com/insights/sustainability/business_society_and_the_future_of_capitalism?cid=other-eml-nsl-mip-mck-oth-1406 , McKinsey Quarterly, May 2014.

Porter, M.E., Heppelman, J.E., "How Smart, Connected Products Are Transforming Competition", Harvard Business Review, November 2014.

Schmidt, E., & Rosenberg, J., "How Google Works", John Murray, 2014.

Schwab, K., "Are you ready for the technological revolution?" World Economic Forum Paper, 19 February 2015.

Shell, "Scenario Planning", http://www.shell-livewire.org/business-library/business-plans/why-you-need-a-business-plan/Scenario-planning/

Shill, W., Engel, J.F., Mann, D., Schatteman, O., Corporate Agility: Six ways to make volatility your friend, Accenture Outlook Journal, No 3, 2012.

Sull, D., "Competing through organizational agility", McKinsey Quarterly, December 2009.

Taleb, N.N., "Fooled by Randomness: The Hidden Role of Chance in Life and in the Markets", 2004.

Taleb, N.N., "The Black Swan: The Impact of the Highly Improbable", 2007.

Tetlock, P., Gardner, D., "Superforecasting – The Art and Science of Prediction", Random House Books, 2015.

Tett, G., "The Silo Effect: Why putting everything in its place isn't such a bright idea", Little Brown, London, 2015.

Tett, G., "Why we no longer trust the experts", The Financial Times Magazine, 1 July 2016.

Thaler, R.H., "Misbehaving: The Making of Behavioural Economics", Penguin, 2015.

The Economist, "Business Strategy and Technology - Big Bang Theory", 11 April 2014.

The Economist, "A Hard Act To Follow", 28 June 2014.

The Times 100 Business Case Studies, "Creating a high performance culture - A Siemens case study": http://businesscasestudies.co.uk/siemens/creating-a-high-performance-culture/talent-management.html#axzz2tlteOnzc

Tomorrow's Company & Mazars, "The Board Charter – Promoting business in society", Consultation Draft, 2014.

Tushman, O'Reilly, "Ambidextrous organizations: Managing evolutionary and revolutionary change", 1996.

Van Alstyne, M.W., Parker, G.G., Choudary, S.P., "Pipelines, Platforms, and the New Rules of Strategy", Harvard Business Review, April 2016.

Williams, T., Worley, C.G., & Lawler., E.G., "The Agility Factor", Strategy + Business, 15 April 2013.

Watkins, M.D., Bazerman, M.H., "Predictable Surprises – The Disasters that you should have seen coming", Harvard Business Review, March 2003.

World Economic Forum Outlook on the Global Agenda http://www.weforum.org/reports/outlook-global-agenda-2014

HUW MORRIS

ABOUT THE AUTHOR

After school in Hertfordshire (just North of London in England), Huw Morris spent 3 years at Physical Education College where a primary interest was coaching Gymnastics and organising International Competitions. He attended the International Olympic Academy in Olympia in 1976 and the World Student Games in Sofia in 1977.

From 1977 to 1993 he served as a Royal Air Force Officer in the United Kingdom, Germany and the United States. Initial appointments in Finance and Human Resources were followed by a number of generalist roles that included Aide de Camp for a Commander-in-Chief and the RAF New Management Strategy Team in the Ministry of Defence. While in the latter role he conducted research into culture change for a dissertation.

Huw graduated with an MBA from Henley Business School in 1993 and after a period of Business School teaching he joined Andersen Consulting in 1996. His appointments included Quality Management, Practice Strategy and Global Industry Programmes for Food & Consumer Goods, Chemicals and Utilities. Following Andersen Consulting becoming Accenture and a Public Company he served as Director of Operations for the Resources Industry Group and as Chief Technology Officer for

Accenture's Swiss based Intellectual property company.

In 2007 Huw joined the then LECG – a NASDAQ listed Finance and Economics Consultancy. He served as European Chief of Staff until FTI Consulting acquired the European assets of the company in 2011. After a period as European Director of HR for FTI Consulting he founded Efficienarta to focus on Executive Development and Corporate Governance Consulting.   Huw qualified as a Chartered Director in 2010.

Huw Morris is married with two boys – aged 24 and 20. His interests include sailing, skiing and cycling (on both a Mountain Bike and a Brompton Folding Bike).

www.ingramcontent.com/pod-product-compliance
Lightning Source LLC
Chambersburg PA
CBHW060545200326
41521CB00007B/491